Areas for Growth

Exercises in Developmental Drama

Jerome Hanratty

Published by the Press Syndicate of the University of Cambridge
The Pitt Building, Trumpington Street, Cambridge, CB2 1RP
40 West 20th Street, New York, NY 10011–4211, USA
10 Stamford Road, Oakleigh, Melbourne 3166, Australia

© Cambridge University Press 1994

First published 1994
Printed in Great Britain by Bell and Bain Ltd., Glasgow

A catalogue record for this book is available from the British Library.

ISBN 0 521 46910 4

Prepared for publication by Paren & Stacey Editorial Consultants
Designed by Geoffrey Wadsley
Edited by Alison Hart

Contents

Introduction

The relationship between drama and self-development has always been close. Through its processes, drama engages the participants in varieties of experience, builds concentration and confidence, and develops physical attributes of voice and body. Personality, which influences behaviour, is also itself influenced by drama: by practical work in human interaction and the forms of communication that lie behind relationships. In a self-developmental way, it can repair weaknesses, introduce positive attributes and strengthen qualities that are already there.

From such an approach, this book attempts to set out vital areas of personality and behaviour which are capable of development towards a stage where they can help the person to form a balanced and significant relationship with other people and with the experiences of life itself. The method is to look specifically at two elements: firstly, the area which can be fostered; secondly, exercises in practical drama that would seem appropriate to help this. There will of course be overlaps. Basic drama work dealing with concentration, sensitivity, involvement and memory can belong to all areas. Individuals differ and life itself cannot so easily be split into sections. However, a system such as this does provide a schematic guide which the teacher can use as a frame of reference.

In the exercises which follow there is a sequential pattern of development from concentration work through bridging improvisations to fuller interaction. The bulk of the material consists of situations which can be structured by using the normal bases of improvisation, in particular the 5 'W's – *Who?* (person), *Where?* (place), *When?* (time), *What?* (action), *Why?* (motivation) – and which should provide further scope for creative development and personal exploration. A further extension includes, in each chapter, a relevant textual reference giving opportunity for relating practical processes to the experience behind the printed word, so that this experience can be recreated when the words leave the page. The questions and suggestions which follow the extracts from *plays* are designed to help the participant bring himself into the thoughts, attitudes and feelings of the speakers, so that when he comes to act the piece their words are his. Those following the *poems* are to help understanding for reading aloud or for related improvisational work.

If they are to have a real effect, the stages of drama mentioned in the previous paragraph need to be worked through so that a child can assimilate each as he develops his understanding of the processes and his ability in them. In other words, he has to learn to involve himself so that his participation is genuine and avoids the superficiality of that type of role-playing where the emphasis is on pretending rather than experiencing. Instead, the weight should be on the individual researching the resources of his own personality to meet various needs and challenges and respond positively to them.

Qualities of personality and behaviour spread themselves indiscriminately, ignoring the familiar divisions of intellect and social background; and this universality makes it less easy to sort the material into neatly separated age ranges. Flexibility is important, therefore, with the teacher selecting and adapting the work to meet variations within the class or group. My own preference for many of these exercises would be to use them with the 13–16 age range (loosely, adolescents), although they can be adapted for younger children (see also the Special Needs Supplement) and I have used a number of them with the 9–12 age group.

Much of the assessment of this sort of work will depend on the knowledge and experience of the participants when evaluating individual development in relation to potential. Indications are given, in the Teaching Notes, of challenges that are posed and achievements that could follow. To this end, I have outlined for each chapter the connections between a diagnostic understanding of each area and its relevant drama elements.

1 Confidence

Description

Confidence – not to be confused with cockiness, flamboyance or exhibitionism – is underpinned by self awareness and self reliance. Challenges and demands, which might otherwise cause anxiety, are looked at and assessed rationally, and related to an understanding of how one can cope.

Progressing towards confidence, one has to conquer the sort of apprehension (of people and of social situations) which shows itself in shyness and timidity (or, at an extreme, in agrophobia and withdrawal), when social skills are undervalued and simple actions over-elaborated because they loom so large. In reaching a state where a person can face and take decisions independently, he or she may go through a stage of aggression (see Chapter 3) where belligerence camouflages the anxiety and stress of change. Successful completion of the journey shows itself in calmness and economy of behaviour.

Drama approach

We can begin to build the confidence of members of a group by providing a series of simple demands which they have to learn not to veer away from. Then we would wish to involve them in a variety of social situations where they can meet and learn to cope with the decisions and challenges which lie there. These will include practice in relating to and addressing other people, basic to which should be an interest *in* other people. At first, the participants need the support of a framework in structuring situations, though they will probably be able to supply their own details within this.

For results and benefits to be lasting, the emphasis should be on a genuine involvement in the experiences of the situation, not the surface operation of procedures and 'skills'. Hence the importance of developing concentration so that the participant can focus fully on the other people in the situation and forget about himself or herself. This should lead, through practice, to a real and outgoing awareness of other people and events in a true perspective.

A final point to note is that, before they become fully self reliant, many of the participants tend to preconceive their actions, that is to behave in a way they think is expected rather than from their own natural volition. Therefore, to help spontaneity, it is useful to present them with unexpected elements and divergent options during the actual improvisations.

A good image 2

Description

To appeal to other people it is necessary first to appeal to oneself. So, self belief can underly behaviour which shows assertion, effort and enterprise. To maintain these consistently, add a sense of purpose so that goals, however small, are deliberately aimed for. The result should be meaningful action rather than, for example, day-dreaming and depression (two characteristics of low self esteem).

If other people are looked at positively, with interest, respect, kindness and acceptance, the attitude reflects on oneself: eliminating the defensiveness of suspicion, mistrust and aggressive criticism – those negative qualities which so often spring from a fear of rejection.

Drama approach

If the work can induce a feeling of security and a basic level of confidence, we can then concentrate on the participants getting more of a grip by becoming aware of what is involved in a situation and how to use themselves in it. Allied with this is the vital need to build up inner resources (see also Chapter 3) rather than indulging in disorganised fantasies (another characteristic of inadequate esteem).

The situations themselves should give scope for firmness, and offer challenges. In particular, there should be contexts for the use of responsibility, leadership and decision making, with role switching showing its value in highlighting variety of approach and, consequently, the variety of resources available. Concentration and memory work is consistently relevant, and practice in physical action (see also Chapter 4) can arouse an aptitude and confidence that go beyond the body.

The chip off the shoulder 3

Description

When putting a point of view, taking part in a discussion or arguing a case, the old parable of the sun and the wind is a relevant one. Strength of mind and ability in action can underly behaviour which seems initially to be aggressive and belligerent; but they can also manifest themselves in less adversarial ways. In confrontations, when problems are to be solved and decisions made, a person who wishes to be co-operative and genuinely looks forward to outcomes is more likely to find the answer and make the appropriate choices than someone blurred by anxiety, suspicion and defensiveness (the classic symptoms of the chip on the shoulder) or the obstacles of frustration, fear and disinterest.

The area of operation is one where responsibility is called for; it includes decision making, weighing up of considerations and opinions, clarity of view, sharing of responsibilities and firmness of action. These are the attributes of an effective member of a team – but also of its successful leader.

Drama approach

The first aim is for the participant to become involved through genuine interest rather than as a mere routine. To kick-start, I have found that using some sort of controversial discussion or provocative topic as an opening can often arouse contrary and forceful views, so that the participants are becoming involved without realising it. This helps subsequent dramatic projection into a basic situation. I have also found it useful in such beginnings to employ a sort of 'devil's advocate' approach, where the 'wrong' view may be attacked simply because the authority figure is upholding it (e.g. a teacher supporting abolition of discipline).

Involvement has three outlets: a channel for those positive qualities that already exist; a pruning or diversion of those which may be over-developed; and an expansion (in character and action) of those which need fostering. There may be times, for instance, when forcefulness and strength of will may seem to suit a leader's role, but at other times, the individual possessing them might be better employed, for personal development, in a subordinate position.

Ideally, some form of discrimination in making decisions and tolerance in making judgements of others is being sought. Situations, therefore, can be structured with this in view and attributes to encourage may well be the opposite of the thrusting stereotype: that is, gentleness, calmness, consideration. Their development can be aided, especially in partner work, by role-switching: to see one's own behaviour, as if in a mirror, in its significance and in perspective.

4 Co-ordination

Description

Development of body skills and fluent, varied movement arises from regular practice in physical co-ordination. But non-physically one can also 'get things together' – and for the benefit of more than the body. Orientation of approach matches consistency of concentration for an alert participation in situations of life, while space awareness can be allied with an enhanced visual and experiental appreciation of form and pattern to give backbone and structure to outlook and activity.

Drama approach

The uses of concentration and structure are a constant priority, as are knowledge of space and awareness of locations (which also act as control factors). Movement work is obviously relevant, to give shape, form and firmness. But the application of movement is not only physical: it can give opportunity for creative disciplining of the imagination and for the structuring of ideas, actions and words in the building up of situations and stories for a co-ordinated use of language and relationships.

Detail is important because, in its promotion of concentration, it is the enemy of that vagueness and mind wandering so often associated with deficient co-ordination. It may be necessary, therefore, to spell out, bit by bit, in small situations, each stage of the action for a slow but gradual opening up of confidence, self awareness and a sense of direction (all fruits of a co-ordinated approach). This sort of tight structuring will need more teacher help and control, with perhaps less scope for the participants initiating and developing their own ideas. However, when they do start producing results on their own and dropping you, then you are starting to win.

Special needs supplement   4a

Lack of co-ordination is a feature often associated with learning difficulties. These may result from specific mental or physical barriers, or from a general deficiency in the ability to concentrate or to relate items towards a logical conclusion and decisive action. The most obvious symptoms are inattention, as the mind wanders off, and incomprehension, as the mind cannot take in or remember what is required. Physical shortcomings reinforce the condition, as a valuable aid to achievement is absent or lacking.

In a drama approach the recipe is the same, but even more so: in other words, a concentration on the basic factors of participation, and a very simplified structuring of their stages. It is, again, necessary to set these out step by step; and, to help individual development, to be alert to the variety of choices and options possible for each action.

As the exercise of co-ordination reaches out to what may be a child's limitations in other areas of growth, much of the work in this and other chapters can be simplified and adapted to meet that extra demand. However, I am appending, in this supplement, a series of related exercises which I have found valuable when working with those who have had particular learning difficulties.

A final note is to indicate that, as some of the participants may have difficulties with reading, the wording of the exercises is designed so that they can also be read aloud to the group.

5 Supporting the feelings

Description

Fear of the feelings may often be at the root of inadequate social behaviour and destructive or negative conduct. Acceptance of them, however, with an understanding of their operation, can aid perception of how individuals 'tick' and people connect. The development of sensitivity and imagination promotes readiness of response which, in turn, helps to deepen emotional experience and make it meaningful. This then provides a base for creativity and positive participation in the non-mechanical side of life.

Drama approach

Here we find ourselves associated with one of the oldest aims of teaching: to enrich an individual's sensibility, so often the province of the arts in education. With drama we would also expect this cultural growth to be associated with social growth by developing the ability to cope independently with the emotional challenges and pressures that will inevitably come.

Although we cannot supply the feelings themselves we can supply contexts in which they operate, giving an opportunity for experiencing their variety, their subtlety and their significant involvement in story building (adventurous and aesthetic) or in situations requiring a range of characters, attitudes and emotions.

In many ways, what we are trying to do is to prepare people for independence (especially imminent school leavers). As with the work done on Confidence and a Good Image, this requires more than an attention to an individual's surface presentation. The root lies deeper and must be cultivated from down there.

6 Making relationships

Description

The secret of making good relationships is to take away the focus from the self and direct it on to others. Contact begins this way and is maintained by developing an interest in the interests of the other person.

But is this person interested in you? Reverse the process mentioned above: just as personality deficiencies (especially introversion) can block development of contacts, so a positive character with a variety of interests will attract the interest of others. A similar variety within personality and behaviour finds its mirror in the establishing and growth of relationships; and underlying are the ability and wish to understand, share and tolerate.

Drama approach

Relationships are basic to drama and crucial to a person's development within it. There is consequently a strong link with all the other areas and particularly with Communication (Chapter 7) and Feelings (Chapter 5).

When we have a relationship with someone, however small it may be, we have a particular attitude to that person and a particular feeling about him or her. So, the way in to successful participation is first to cultivate a genuine interest in the person and then to become involved in a way that brings in the feelings and attitudes that are required. Scope therefore is needed for a variety of situations containing a mixture of characters and emotions, and giving opportunity for working reciprocally together.

This should provide a corresponding variety in the functions of personality, and here it is important to avoid someone staying too exclusively in the type of role that best suits his or her own nature. In particular, we should provide subservient and helping functions for the over-dominant individual or bully (both of them illustrative of difficulty in relating satisfactorily). In this way, they might more easily see their own behaviour, in its significance, from another angle.

Finally, it is important to avoid the clichéd or over-familiar type of relationship being projected. This is best achieved by letting relationships form and be discovered through the character interaction rather than imposing them beforehand. So the drama creates the relationship.

Communication 7

Description

The foundations of good communication are physical and literal: we think of someone who is audible and articulate, with flow and variety in language. Beyond these basic adequacies, however, are qualities of listening and understanding. Ideas need to be economically structured and points of view effectively expressed. Just as a deprived personality or background can restrict communication, so extended horizons can increase the motivation for it as well as its range. Motivation to communicate can also override lack of words. Day-dreaming, excessive introspection and, extremely, autism might be regarded as side effects of poor communication – but something is there to be tapped.

Drama approach

Because this area is so relevant to all others, a wide use of all drama elements is appropriate; almost every exercise so far would suit. In particular, however, we would wish to employ situations giving specific scope for language variety and for listening that is receptive but also creative (so that what is heard can be bounced back in a relevant response). Listening skills will include an awareness of posture, eye contact, and a knowledge of when to intrude, when to keep silent and when to restrain one's own opinions (note, too, remarks on interview organisation in Chapter 1). Practice in non-verbal communication and relevant voice exercises are initial or accompanying stages in the whole process, but basic to all is a stress on motivation – to stimulate the desire and need to communicate – and the fostering of an outgoing interest in other people and in life itself.

8   Social growth

Description

When we look at personal growth we cannot avoid also viewing its field of operation. Social growth, both the outlet and development of a person's maturing, will need therefore to be seen within a framework of social situations. Many of these will have occurred in previous chapters relevant to specific areas and, in general, life provides a varied set of contexts. These give scope for an interlinked use of personality characteristics in a mutually influential way but with an underlying base: the operation of a person in society.

Society has its problems: presenting challenges and demands to an individual, who may, or may not, be able to cope. The problems can be found in the structures of the society itself – its laws, taboos, customs, rankings, etc. – or may be caused by other people and the individual himself interpreting those structures and behaving in a particular manner within them. Either way, the pressures usually have urgency of concern for young people in their learning rise and can bring difficulties. Failure to overcome those difficulties means that the problems continue through adult life; success enables progress towards the next step: responsibility.

Drama approach

The work in one way needs to widen, because it may include many or most of the areas of personality and behaviour already dealt with. In another way it might be narrower because the focus of operation will often be more closely confined. Participation through a drama involvement (as opposed to 'simulation'), should both highlight the reality underlying the situations and provide its experience. What follows – how the individual tries to find a satisfactory resolution – will depend on one's own personality and how this measures up to the options that will be available. Qualities of personality will have been investigated in the previous chapters – so how an individual knows his or her capabilities will point to the ways in which these are used to find a solution that suits.

There may be no easy answer (and maybe no one answer at all). Not understanding this can be a danger for those taking part (looking for the glib solution and quick-fix method). A similar diversion might be the potential of the exercises for discussion rather than action (discussion coming at a later stage, consequent upon whatever decisions were taken). Too much attention might be given to the social framework itself; instead we should be looking at the strength of the individual's reliance and ability to cope within that framework. Ultimately, the reward of the work is not in the airing it gives to a topic (valuable though that may be) but in the effect it has on the participant's own outlook and behaviour.

1 To begin with

1 This is a very simple introduction to concentration and sharing work. The participants are learning to respond; developing the response should put the participant more at ease and help relaxation.

2 This exercise is designed to encourage inventive thinking. It should make the participants aware of divergencies and steer them away from pre-conceiving. If the participants are shy to begin with, one can start with a discussion and lead into action, but it is better the other way round. Emphasis should be on the individual discovering 'why', but if the exercise is done in groups of three it helps to get different opinions and stimulus from other people.

3 This exercise makes demands on the imagination, and challenges participants to speak out, with the mind and memory researching on itself to build confidence. a)–e) involve an individual speaking to a group, but f)–j) are better done as pair work, or as individual to teacher.

Note that f)–j) are literal (i.e. a dream you actually had) to encourage involvement in the reality of recollected experience.

4 This is about getting in tune with another person's actions, attitudes, thoughts and feelings to develop concentration, and the ability to work together and should take away any pre-occupation with self. As involvement increases you often find the participant manipulating the partner; creating the actions as well as commenting on them. Note that this is also a test for the partner: ultimately, how closely can the two correspond?

5 This exercise tests the interviewer's ability to organise his or her thoughts and words and to become interested and involved with the other person. It will also test how inventive and imaginative the interviewee can be.

As the interviews proceed, in this and other exercises, there is scope for reference to more overt interviewing skills: eye contact; the use of short, relevant questions (which avoid too many yes or no answers), and of 'leading' or provocative ones; the selection of material in an organised plan; allowing the interviewee the freedom to talk, without interruption, but keeping to the point; the importance of impartiality (keeping one's own views out of it unless deliberately to stimulate a response); and awareness of openings for further questions.

To begin with

1 Try these exercises in a group:

a) one member makes up a fairly long descriptive sentence; it is then passed round the group as a whispered message

b) one member makes up a short sentence; the next member repeats the sentence, then adds something of his own to it, and so on...

c) pass an imaginary object round the group; it keeps changing

d) do word association round the group

e) each member tries to touch as many of the other group members as possible, without being touched

2 A person returns to the house after a day at work and tries the key in the lock. Nothing happens. Can you think of five or more:

a) reasons for this

b) courses of action he or she would immediately take

c) others who could be involved

d) follow-ups

e) other main characters (i.e. not someone returning from work) or other locations (i.e. not the house)

Enact any of these situations.

3 Study an imaginary:

a) letter, then read aloud from it

b) menu, then order from it

c) set of instructions, then tell the rest of a group

d) map (or bus timetable), then give directions for a journey

e) address of welcome, then read it to an important visitor

Reveal to your partner or group:

f) a dream

g) an ambition

h) a secret wish – for yourself, then for others

i) the description of another person

j) your ideal holiday

4 Give an exact descriptive commentary on the actions of a person as he or she is doing them. These can be:

a) everyday actions (e.g. rising from a chair or opening a window)

b) actions in an imaginary situation (e.g. getting ready for a party, but not being able to find your shoes)

When you are used to this, try including in the commentary the thoughts that might be running through the person's head as he or she is doing the actions. Could any of the actions be the start of a further situation or story (e.g. searching in a cellar and finding...)?

5 Interview the following people:

a) a taxi driver who witnessed a crime

b) someone about their views on a current topic

c) a friend who has just returned from holiday

d) the driver of a school bus

e) a lonely police officer

f) the owner of a restaurant regularly visited by famous people

g) someone about why he or she became a...

h) someone who has lost their job

i) the boss of your local radio station

Wanted for TV

This provides practice in the use of detail needed for a dramatised situation and in creating awareness of varying outcomes and approaches (which will help to break away from pre-conceiving).

The sections on *Preparation* and *To think about* provide guidelines on how the situation can be broken down, then built up and given body for the participants' greater depth and involvement.

The basic situation is the interview itself, testing how confidently an individual can present himself in a situation where stress is present and demands are made. Panellists are safe in the framework of a structure, a useful introduction for someone not yet ready, in drama terms, for exposure.

Then work over the improvisation for practice and for development. What can be found out through this? For instance, can the students discover, through trial and error, the by-products of effective presentation (for example posture, body language, positive replies), in an interview situation?

Follow-up

a) This can be very revealing: the presenter doesn't always find it as easy as was imagined. There is scope for extra work in building up practice in confident action (more use of the interviews from previous page can help here).

b) This is a test of independence in thought, with the emphasis on individual volition.

c) A situation can be set up for this (e.g. phoning home after the interview) where reactions and conversations are not stereotyped but are motivated and arise naturally from the situation.

d and e) These are extra situations relevant to what has been done, the benefits of which should show in new inventiveness and detail.

Wanted for TV

Interviews are being held for the post of presenter on a local TV station. There are four candidates and four members on the panel, one of whom is chairperson.

Preparation

a) Each candidate writes down details of qualifications, experience, interests, etc., and these can be studied by the panel before the interview.
b) Each member of the panel should think about his or her background. A TV executive? A local journalist? A local councillor?
c) What is the role and background of the chairperson? Will he or she have strong views about the post or be neutral?
d) What are the panellists and the candidates likely to talk about before the interviews start?

To think about

a) What type of questions would be relevant? Would there be a practical test?
b) In addition to qualifications and experience, what other qualities are the panel looking for? What kind of personality?
c) How important are the voice and physical appearance of the candidate likely to be?
d) How should the candidates dress and behave to appear to the best advantage?

Follow-up

a) The new TV presenter is in action: devise an activity or item to show this.
b) Three other TV jobs, of a different nature, are offered to the other candidates. Will they accept?
c) What are the reactions and conversations which follow the interviews?
d) One of the panel members is accused of favouritism.
e) Try some other job-interview situations:
   • youth club leader
   • disc-jockey
   • travel courier
   • salesman
   • receptionist

And to follow

As with so many drama situations, these can be done in pairs or groups with all the class working at once. When the participants feel strong enough, then particular groups can be looked at by the class as a whole.

In general the guided structuring of the previous section (particularly the variety of outcomes available) can be applied here. Help may be needed at first with ideas and structuring: when participants can do more of this themselves, their confidence is increasing.

1 This is about engaging oneself constructively with others. With both partners, the fabrication of a need for help can take attention away from their own preoccupations. It begins with simple conversation and progresses to wider action where more demands are made. Encourage participants to take their time over reading the letter, so that they can concentrate and for the words to become actual and real to the mind.

2 Here there is involvement in basic encounters where confidence is needed. Demands are made first on conversation, then on action. Check if eye contact is being made: often it is missing where there is a lack of confidence. It cannot be forced but can be encouraged. If there are difficulties, try stimulating the participant's interest in, and curiosity about, the other people. This can help overcome shyness in life situations, for example meeting strangers at a party, especially if you are the odd one out.

3 The initial exercise of sitting in a chair and opening a door is more than it seems: a drama exercise in itself, giving opportunities for concentration and fitting oneself into a state of mind and action. This gets the senses and the body right.

It then progresses into situations which may require extra confidence and which could lead into a story. Note the hints in a)–e) on structuring (the 5 'W's) and the probable need for assertion by the individual. Progress is made if this can be done effectively. Initially, the exercises will be individual ones (focusing on the mind, thinking and feeling), then each can develop into pair or group work.

It can then develop with the more detailed options of f)–j): more deliberation can be given to building in a variety of incidents and characters, looking at motivation and details of background.

4 This is a deliberately lengthy development of a relationship which demands specific initiatives from both sides; for example the social worker is challenged if the prisoner refuses to talk or becomes aggressive. It is interesting to see if the relationship changes when moving from a) to b) because of the different circumstances, and if its overall development helps confidence.

There is opportunity for story in e) and it is interesting to see if the police are called: I have rarely known it happen when doing this exercise.

5 This shows the development and variations possible in stress situations, and gives practice in resourcing oneself to overcome them. The encounters can be simple short ones or can be filled out to more complex situations. It is important in the more extended situations that decisions taken by the participants are honest and their attitudes real: not doing it as they think it 'should be done', which can look impressive but is of little value to the individual's development. For example in i) the innocence of the person is more likely to be genuine if he or she is out of the room when the initial complaints, eye-witness accounts etc. are made.

BILLY LIAR

BILLY. Well, what about me? Don't you think I worry? I worry about the H-bomb. You didn't know I nearly went on the Aldermaston march last Easter, did you? I don't want another war, you know. And what about all them refugees? You never stop to consider them, do you? Or South Africa. (*At which point* RITA *makes up her mind, and, without knocking, marches into the house and into the living-room.*) Do you know, Barbara, if you were a blackie and we lived in South Africa I'd be in gaol by now? Doing fifteen years. (*At which point he breaks off as* RITA *makes her entrance.*) Hallo, Rita.

RITA (*to* BILLY, *indicating* ALICE). It takes her some time to come out of the lavatory, doesn't it? What's she been doing? Writing her will out?

ALICE (*outraged*). Do you usually come into people's houses without knocking?

RITA. I do when people have got my private property. (*To* BILLY.) Come on—give.

BILLY. Rita, I don't think you've ever met my mother, have you?

RITA. No, but she'll know me again, won't she? Come on, you and your stinking rotten jewellers. I'm not daft, you know.

ALICE (*shocked*). We're not having this! Where does she think she is?

BILLY (*attempting to guide* RITA *towards the door he takes her elbow*). I'll just take Rita as far as the bus stop, mother.

RITA (*shrugging him away*). Take your mucky hands off me, you rotten toffee-nosed get. You didn't think I'd come in, did you?

ALICE. No, but I think you'll go out, young lady. And if you've anything to say to my son you'd better just remember where you are.

BILLY. Well, I'm very glad you have come, Rita, because I feel I owe you a word of explanation.

RITA (*imitating him*). Oooh, I feel I owe you a word of explanation. Get back in the cheese, with the other maggots.

ALICE. I'm not putting up with this—I shall bring his father down.

RITA. You can bring his rotten father down. I hope you do. And his rotten grandma.

BARBARA. Billy's grandma, for your information, happens to be ill in bed.

RITA (*turning to* BARBARA *for the first time*). Oooh, look what the cat's brought in. Get Madam Fancy-knickers. I suppose this is your rotten sister. I thought she was supposed to be in a rotten iron lung.

BARBARA. For your information, I happen to be Billy's fiancée.

RITA (*imitating* BARBARA). Oooh, for your information. Well, for your information, he happens to be engaged to me. In front of a witness.

BILLY. How do you mean? What's witnesses got to do with it?

BARBARA. Billy, will you kindly tell me who this girl is?

RITA (*imitating her*). Oooh, Billy, will you kindly tell me? Aw, go take a long walk on a short pier, you squint-eyed sow, you're nothing else.

ALICE. Barbara, would you kindly go upstairs and ask Mr. Fisher to come down for a minute?

RITA. You can fetch him down. Fetch all the rotten lot down. You can fetch the cowing iron lung down as well, for all I care.

ALICE. I've never been spoken to like this in all my days.

BARBARA. Shall I go up, Mrs. Fisher?

RITA (*imitating her*). Oooh, shall I go up, Mrs. Fisher? If you can get up the stairs with them bow legs, you can.

ALICE. It's all right, Barbara. I'll deal with this young madam. I've met her type before.

BILLY. I think I can explain all this.

BARBARA. Yes, I think you've got some explaining to do, Billy.

RITA. He can explain until he's blue in the rotten face. It makes no difference to me.

ALICE. If I knew your mother, young lady, wouldn't I have something to say to her.

RITA. You can keep out of this. It's between me and him. (*To* BILLY.) Where's my ring? Has she got it? (BARBARA's *right hand instinctively goes to her left.*) She has, hasn't she? You've given it to her, haven't you?

BILLY. Ah, well—yes, but you see . . . Only there's been a bit of a mix-up. You see, I thought Barbara had broken the engagement off.

BARBARA. Billy!

RITA. Yeh, well you've got another think coming if you think I'm as daft as she is. You gave that ring to me. And don't think you can go crawling out of it, 'cause you can't. You seem to forget I've got a witness, you know. I've got two. 'cause Shirley Mitchem saw you giving me it, as well—so you needn't think she didn't. I can go down to the Town Hall, you know.

ALICE. Now, don't you come running in here with them tales, my girl. You know as well as I do he's under age.

RITA. Ask him if he was under age down at Foley Bottoms last night. 'cause I'm not carrying the can back for nobody. He wasn't under-age then. He was over-age more like.

ALICE. Get out! Get out of my house!

BARBARA. Have you been untrue to me, Billy? I've got to know.

RITA (*imitating her*). Oooh, have you been untrue to me, Billy! Get out of your push-chair, babyface. (*To* BILLY.) You're just rotten, aren't you? You are—you're rotten, all through. I've met some people in my time, but of all the lying, scheming . . . anyway, you gave that ring to me.

BILLY. Yes, but, look, Rita . . .

RITA (*interrupting*). Don't talk to me, you rotten get. Well, she can have you—if she knows what to do with you, which I very much doubt. You rotten lying get. Garr—you think you're somebody, don't you? But you're nobody. You miserable lying rotten stinking get.

BILLY. Does this mean you're breaking off our engagement?

RITA. You don't get out of it like that. I want that ring.

BARBARA (*finding the right word at last*). Billy, have you been—having relations with this girl?

RITA (*swinging round on* BARBARA). What do you think he's been doing? Knitting a pullover? You know what you can do, don't you? You can give me that ring. Because it's mine.

ALICE. If you don't stop it this minute! (*To* BILLY.) As for you, I hope you know what you've done, because I don't.

RITA. Are you going to give me that ring?

BARBARA. I shall give the ring back to Billy—if and when I break off the engagement.

BILLY (*moving towards her*). Barbara.

RITA. Yes, you can go to her. She can have you. And she knows what she can do, the squint-eyed, bow-legged, spotty, snotty-nosed streak of nothing.

BARBARA. And you know what you can do as well. You can wash your mouth out with soap and water.

RITA (*imitating*). Oooh, you can wash your mouth out with soap and water. You could do with some soap in your ears, you've got carrots growing out of them. Well, you can give me that ring. Before I come over there and get it.

ALICE. You can get out of this house. I won't tell you again.

RITA. Save your breath for blowing out candles. I want my ring. (*Crossing towards* BARBARA.) Yes, and I'm going to get it.

ALICE. Get out of my house! Get out! Get out!

(GEOFFREY FISHER *emerges from the bedroom and comes slowly down the stairs.*)

RITA (*moving right up to* BARBARA). Are you going to give me that ring, or aren't you?

GEOFFREY (*half-way down the stairs*). Mother! . . . Mother!
RITA. Because you'll be in Emergency Ward Ten if I don't get it—
right sharpish.
BARBARA. Don't you threaten me.
RITA. I won't threaten you—I'll flatten you! Give me that cowing
ring back! (*She makes a grab for* BARBARA'S *hand*.)
BARBARA (*pushing her away*). I won't . . . I won't. . . .
ALICE. Will you stop it, the pair of you!
GEOFFREY (*enters the room and stands in the doorway. He appears not to
comprehend what is happening*). Mother!

>(GEOFFREY'S *word silences* ALICE, BILLY *and* BARBARA *who turn
and look at him*.)

RITA (*unconcerned*). Give me the ring!
GEOFFREY. You'd better come upstairs. Come now. I think she's dead.

THE CURTAIN FALLS.

ACT THREE

Later the same evening.

It is about half-past nine and quite dark in the garden outside the FISHERS' *house. When the action of the play takes place in the garden, however, a street lamp comes up from the road beyond the garden and off-stage. There is also a small light in the porch of the house. As the curtain rises* GEOFFREY FISHER *is going through the contents of* BILLY'S *cupboard which are, at the moment, spread across the floor of the living-room by the sideboard.* ALICE FISHER *is sitting in a chair by the fire. She is obviously distraught by the death of her mother.* GEOFFREY *rummages through the envelopes and papers and then rises, shaking his head.*

GEOFFREY. Well, I can't bloody find it. It's not in here, anyway. He hasn't got it. It's about the only bloody thing he hasn't got.

ALICE. She might not have had one, Geoffrey—you know what she was like.

GEOFFREY (*although he hasn't changed his vocabulary there is a more tender note than usual in his voice*). Don't talk so bloody wet, lass. Everybody's got a birth certificate.

ALICE. Well, you don't know, Geoffrey, they might not have had them in those days. She was getting on.

GEOFFREY. Everybody's got a bloody birth certificate. They've had them since the year dot. If he's got it squat somewhere I'll bloody mark him for life.

ALICE. You can't blame our Billy for everything, Geoffrey. What would he want with it?

GEOFFREY (*indicating the papers on the floor*). What's he want with this bloody lot? There's neither sense nor bloody reason in him. And where is he, anyway? Where's he taken himself off to?

ALICE. I don't know, Geoffrey. I've given up caring.

GEOFFREY. You'd think he could stay in one bloody night of the year. He ought to be in tonight. He ought to be in looking after his mother. He's got no sense of bloody responsibility, that's his trouble.

ALICE. Well, she liked her cup of tea. We'll have that pint-pot to put away now. She's used that pint-pot for as long as I can remember.

GEOFFREY. She liked her bloody tea, there's no getting away from it. (*He half-jokes in an attempt to lift* ALICE *out of her depression.*) If I had a shilling for every pot of tea she's supped I'd be a rich man today. Well, there's one good thing to be said for it, when does the dustbin man come around? 'cause he can take all them tins of condensed milk out of her bedroom.

ALICE. We can't throw them away. Somebody might be glad of them. We could send them round to the Old People's Home, or something.

GEOFFREY. Get away with you, you'd poison the bloody lot of them. That stuff doesn't keep for ever you know. They'll be green mouldy.

ALICE. I thought it was supposed to keep—condensed milk.

GEOFFREY. It won't keep twenty bloody years, I'm sure. She's had that pile of tins stacked up there since nineteen thirty-nine. And there's not one of them been opened—not one.

ALICE. Well, they went scarce, Geoffrey, when the war started, you know. That's why she started saving them.

GEOFFREY. Went scarce? Too bloody true they went scarce, she had them all. She hoarded them—she was like a squirrel with them. If Lord Woolton had heard about her in nineteen forty-one she'd have got fifteen years. By bloody hell, she would. (*He reminisces gently.*) Hey! I say! Do you remember how I used to pull her leg about it? How I used to tell her the food office was ringing up for her? You couldn't get her near that bloody telephone. She used to let it ring when we were out—she must have lost me pounds.

ALICE (*not cheered by* GEOFFREY'S *attempt at humour*). Well, I only hope you manage as well when you're as old as she was. She's not had an easy life—I wish I could have made it easier for her. She had all us to bring up, you know. And that took some doing.

GEOFFREY. No—she didn't do too bad, to say. What was she? Eighty-what?

ALICE. She'd have been eighty-three in August. Either eighty-three or eighty-two. She didn't seem to know herself.

GEOFFREY. Well, I shan't grumble if I last as long—she had a fair old crack of the whip.

ALICE. She didn't suffer, that's something to be grateful for. Some of them hang on for months and months. What did you say she was talking about? Before she went?

GEOFFREY. Don't ask me. I couldn't hear for that bloody shambles that

And to follow

1 A letter contains bad news: perhaps a disappointment. Tell it to a friend. Can he or she give help and comfort? Now reverse the situation: the letter contains good news – perhaps a pleasant surprise. Can your friend share in this?

Now meet the person who wrote the bad/good news.

Try these 'help' situations:
a) you are 'on the run', asking someone for help
b) a phone call, someone asking for help
c) a friend is in difficulties
d) someone needs help in the workshop
e) a citizen needs help

2 You are meeting new people. What do you do when:
a) showing them round the school
b) explaining the machinery to foreign visitors
c) meeting strangers at a party
d) arriving at a youth hostel
e) taking a Saturday job

3 Sit on a chair, open a door, when:

a) waiting outside the Head teacher's room (why?)
b) expecting an important visitor to call (who?)
c) during a robbery (where?)
d) having received good (or bad) news (what?)
e) on an important day in your life (when?)

Try these other door-opening situations:

f) a neighbour is complaining
g) your caller has unwelcome news
h) a salesman has an attractive offer

i) someone unexpected is in the room
j) you are applauded

4 A trainee social-worker is chatting with a prisoner for the first time, trying to find out the prisoner's background, opinions, personality, etc. and to give help by listening and talking.

The stages in their relationship are:
a) the prisoner is to be released in two weeks' time
b) five weeks later, a chance meeting takes place
c) the prisoner is taken home for tea
d) two days later, the social worker returns home early to find the former prisoner going through a chest of drawers

What happens next?

5 You are in the following situations:

a) an encounter when going to school, perhaps on the bus
b) late for an appointment after school
c) shopping for clothes for an important occasion
d) finishing a meal or taking off your make-up while others are watching
e) owning up, and/or apologising
f) asking a favour, or refusing one
g) explaining why the job was not done
h) trying to understand, but others are impatient
i) you are innocent, but are interviewed for an offence
j) you do not want to join in, but find it hard to say 'no'

The breakthrough

At the end of *Roots*, Beatie has reached a level where confidence and assurance are matched by an ability to talk with fluency and interest. From that position, she *wants* to talk and *knows* what she is talking about.

Speech 1 (Lines 1–27) shows she has been helped in this by overcoming earlier difficulties under the influence of Ronnie. A recollection of this influence, of Ronnie's words and actions, must be real to the girl as she speaks, and this memory leads to her own conclusions on the function of language (in her question to Jimmy).

It is important to be aware, however, that Beatie is not talking in a vacuum or to the world in general. She is addressing members of her own family and wanting to convince them. They help her by providing a contrast and also (through the outlook they represent) a target. But, more than that, they are *listeners*; and the quality of listening they provide, how genuinely they follow her words and respond to them, is an essential function in the extract. The scene, therefore, is not just a solo performance.

The final support to Beatie's confidence comes from the words of her last speech (Lines 30–68): they indicate her main targets and reflect her new belief in the deeper values which motivate her attack. The participant must believe in these values; working on the words will tell her why she does.

The breakthrough

In the first extract, Beatie Bryant, a young woman, is telling her sister and brother in law (Jenny and Jimmy) about her fiancé, Ronnie. At the end of the play (second extract), she is shocked when Ronnie sends her a letter finishing their relationship. However, his influence remains as she speaks out to the rest of the family.

1 **Beatie** . . . I was in between jobs and I didn't think to ask for my unemployment benefit. He told me to. But when I asked they told me I was short on stamps and so I wasn't entitled to benefit. I didn't know what to say but he did. *He* went up and argued for me – he's just like his mother, she argues with everyone – and I got it. *I* didn't know how to talk, see, it was all foreign to me. Think of it! An English girl born and bred and I couldn't talk the language – except to buy food and clothes. And sometimes when he were in a black mood he'd start on me. 'What can you talk of?' he'd ask. 'Go and pick a subject. Talk. Use the language. Do you know what language is?' Well, I'd never thought before – hev you? – it's automatic to you isn't it, like walking? 'Well, language is words' he'd say, as though he were telling me a secret.'It's bridges, so that you can get safely from one place to another. And the more bridges you know about the more places you can see!' *(to Jimmy)* And do *you* know what happens when you can see a place but you don't know where the bridge is?

Jimmy *(Angrily)* Blust, gal, what the hell are you on about!

2 **Beatie** . . . You don't want to take any notice of what them ole papers say about the workers bein' all important these days – that's all squit! 'Cos we aren't. Do you think when the really talented people in the country get to work they get to work

for us? Hell if they do! . . . 'Blust,' they say, 'the masses is too stupid for us to come down to them. Blust,' they say, 'if they don't make no effort why should we bother?' So you know who come along? The slop singers and the pop writers and the film makers and women's magazines and the Sunday papers and the picture strip love stories – that's who come along, and you don't have to make no effort for them, it comes easy. 'We know where the money lie,' they say, 'hell we do! The workers've got it so let's give them what they want. If they want slop songs and film idols we'll give 'em that then. If they want words of one syllable, we'll give 'em that then. If they want the third rate, BLUST! We'll give 'em THAT then. Anything's good enough for them 'cos they don't ask for no more!' The whole stinkin' commercial world insults us and we don't care a damn. Well, Ronnie's right – it's our own bloody fault. We want the third rate – we got it! We got it! We . . .

(Suddenly, Beatie stops as if listening to herself. She pauses, turns with an ecstatic smile on her face)

D'you hear that? D'you hear it? Did you listen to me? I'm talking. Jenny, Frankie, mother – I'm not quoting no more . . . RONNIE! It does work . . . It's happening to me . . . I'm beginning, on my own two feet – I'm beginning!

(Arnold Wesker: *Roots*, Acts 1 and 3)

Questions/suggestions

a) and b) Include improvisational work to re-create the past and the reality and influence of Ronnie. This powers Beatie during the speech and forms the picture she is trying to give her listeners. There is a contrast between him and her, during which her own personality begins to show itself.

c) Note where the question suggests that Beatie herself had strong qualities which only needed bringing to the surface. Ronnie therefore can be seen as a catalyst.

d) The play was first produced in 1959, but Beatie's accusations are still relevant today. The improvisatory argument should strengthen the assertiveness of the person playing Beatie.

e) As Beatie's self confidence has awakened she has gone beyond Ronnie and no longer needs him. She is speaking with her own voice.

Finally the participants could be encouraged to look at the other two plays of the Wesker trilogy (*Chicken Soup with Barley* and *I'm talking about Jerusalem*) for further information about Ronnie. This might prompt interesting reflections on the relative development of the two characters and perhaps suggest a further look at the strength of Beatie's own background.

Questions/suggestions

a) When Beatie is talking of Ronnie, how does she want the others to see him? Is her picture wholly complimentary?

b) Devise a scene where Beatie asks for her unemployment benefit, *before* and *after* Ronnie has spoken to her about it. As Ronnie, help Beatie prepare herself for a similar situation.

c) Ronnie would 'start on me' when he 'were in a black mood', but what might be Beatie's reaction, and how might the argument, or row, proceed and end? Try it.

d) Can you think of examples to back up the accusations Beatie is making in her final speech? Devise a scene where Beatie argues these points with a public relations officer from the record industry.

e) Beatie had been stunned when she heard that Ronnie had left her. Why does this not show in her final speech?

2 To begin with

1 The participant should consider the details given while doing the jobs, As a result concentration and depth of involvement should take the action beyond the surface of occupational mime. Sensory and mental perception work together to heighten alertness.

2 This is an exercise for individuals, with firmness of action and voice translated into situations. Can the two match? It is particularly suitable for younger children.

Examples could be: looking for a lost ball; moving from swamp to firm ground; sending someone out of the room; hearing a message; smelling a leak; waking to a warning.

In each exercise one is progressing to a firmness, but the firmness should first be in the mind, and this needs a reason. For variation, try reversing the exercises; for example, moving from confidence to caution.

3 This exercise encourages leadership. Can the organisation be done correctly and efficiently and with some imagination? If so, this should boost self esteem.

4 The interviews relate to occupations, to encourage the participants to think about the detail and background of a person, both as interviewer and interviewee. As confidence and ease improve, extra detail can be invented to extend and deepen the drama situation; for example, suppose the caretaker had recently been shot at?

Notes on interviewing in Chapter 1 (*To begin with* Exercise 5) are relevant to these and to all other interviews in the book.

5 This exercise incorporates imaginative mime and involvement in situations where definite functions operate. It helps the participant's own structuring in outlook and action. As practice in this increases, so should relevant detail. This is a sign of progress.

If the chair is seen as a meaningful part of each situation, this should help participants to develop the characters and their behaviour.

To begin with

1 Imagine you are sweeping a path. Concentrate on and remember:
   a) the size, weight, condition and feel of the brush
   b) the type of path, and what is around (and who?)
   c) what you can hear and smell, etc.
   d) why you are sweeping the path, and when
   e) what is running through your mind while you are doing it

Bring similar detail into the following actions:

   f) dragging a heavy weight
   g) fishing
   h) stacking a shelf
   i) tidying a room
   j) making OR mending something

2 Turn the following physical exercises into drama situations:
   a) look in all directions then fix your eyes firmly on one spot and go to it
   b) step very cautiously, get firmer in your walk and stride out confidently
   c) whisper, then speak hesitantly and build up to a firm steady voice
   d) do not listen, then half listen, and finally listen intently
   e) lie, stretch, crouch, then spring up

3 Organise the following:

   a) a game of musical chairs
   b) a game of your own devising
   c) a tableau
   d) a timetable for a sporting or charity event
   e) a re-arrangement inside a store

4 Imagine you are these people in an interview:
   a) a park keeper
   b) a shop assistant
   c) a car mechanic
   d) a seaman
   e) a lorry driver
   f) a stall holder
   g) a nurse
   h) a tennis player
   i) a film-maker
   j) a school caretaker

5 Without speaking, show your partner that on a chair there is:
   a) a mouse
   b) a pin
   c) a £5 note
   d) 10 marbles
   e) a jagged piece of glass

Your partner gets rid of the object. Now use the chair in the following situations:

   f) waitress to customer
   g) dentist to patient
   h) receptionist to visitor
   i) typist to boss
   j) pupil to teacher

21

Trouble with the boss

As in the previous chapter, the situation can be broken down and built up into mini situations as the teacher sees appropriate.

Development

The role of the manager is to provide a challenge for the waiter or waitress to meet; but the manager also has other demands on him or her, especially in decision making. How each copes is a test of personality development.

Similarly, within the waitress' or waiter's role there can be variations in attitude which should significantly change each enactment of the situation.

Variations

In working out the above options, much will depend on the personalities of the two participants and their relationship. As these can vary, so will the development. Therefore, further changes, calling on new resources, are found in this section. The more subtle and complex the relationships and situations become, the more the personalities of the participants should be developing and the less likelihood there is of stereotyped playing.

Trouble with the boss

A waitress (or waiter) has been summoned to the manager's office because of complaints from one group of diners (about what?). The manager has recently been appointed to improve the place. The waitress has been there for ten months and there have been no previous complaints about her. The diners are important customers.

Development

There are a number of options for the manager.
a) Should the manager try to find the truth. Who is he or she to believe?
b) What action should be taken, if any?
c) What does the manager think or feel about the employee? Will this influence his or her decision?
d) How will the manager cope with any come-back from the waitress?

The waitress also has a number of options.
a) She knows she is innocent, and defends herself.
b) She knows she is innocent, but she is afraid of losing the job. So, how far will she stick up for herself?
c) The complaints were justified. Why? Will she defend herself? How?
d) Guilty or not guilty, she hates the job and the manager and, anyway, is leaving next week for something better.

Variations

a) The waitress is a close friend of the manager's own boss.
b) She has previously done the manager a favour,
c) She was recently extremely insolent to the manager.
d) The manager is afraid of appearing weak.
e) The manager finds her attractive (and she him?)

And to follow

1 Work out details for this exercise beforehand so that each partner has sufficient material to think about. Participants may need help to devise details of the situation, especially for 2 and to establish contexts using the 5 'W's'.

2 This shows what use can be made of reasoned arguments and of the participant's own personal approach? A commitment to the point the persuader is making can build strength of personality and confidence; but, the situations being what they are, both partners can benefit. It will be interesting to note whether the persuader reassures his or her partner.

3 This exercise gives participants an opportunity to assert their views and judgements, and to appreciate and explore those of others. Instead of copying other opinions participants learn that their own opinions can be strengthened by the interchange. Conflict situations can arise; we often shy away from these but feel better and achieve some satisfaction if we do put our point of view. Note, that it is not always easy to keep calm when someone is accusing you or to persist when someone is blocking you. It is necessary to do both however. Watch out for instances of over-assertiveness or aggressiveness, which can be symptoms of poor self esteem.

Use role-switching to help exploration and when fuller situations are emerging, make sure participants decide clearly about who, when, where, why, what, to build up the detail and structure of the situation and help involvement.

4 These are exercises in personal initiative and decision making; but behind them lies personal judgement, not crude authority. In each situation there should be sound reasons for the decisions taken.

5 More responsibility, and perhaps deeper thought, is required in this exercise because of the personal dilemmas that may be present (if one is sufficiently involved). Note carefully, therefore, whether decisions taken are genuine and honest.

The exercises in f)–j) are tests in coping with surprise situations. These will be more effective if the participant does not know beforehand of the mistake or change.

And to follow

1 Try to persuade these people:

 a) a reluctant pupil to leave the class
 b) a bored friend to accompany you
 c) a busy person to do a job
 d) someone you usually don't get on with to do you a favour
 e) an industrialist to open a factory in your area

2 Can you reassure the following people?

 a) Julie, who has bought an expensive piece of jewellery (or clothing) but now has doubts about it
 b) Tom, who has had a bad game
 c) Dave, who feels he will not make a good impression at the party
 d) Carol, who thinks she has hurt your feelings (how?)
 e) Hannah, who fears she will not do well at the interview

3 You have to consider another person's point of view. What do you do when:
 a) someone starts by being rude to you
 b) you complain about some goods that are below standard
 c) you are short-changed
 d) two friends each think the other is the best one to...?
 e) you have to arbitrate over differing views from the group

4 As the manager of a team, defend a decision you have made:
 a) to your best player – why he or she has been dropped
 b) to the Press – your tactics in a game that you lost
 c) to a young beginner – why you think he or she has no future

 d) to an angry player – why you are taking disciplinary action
 e) to the team – why you took that disciplinary action

5 What would you do in these situations?

 a) your friend has run away and asked you not to tell; the parents question you
 b) a part-time job is affecting your school work; the school wants you to give it up, but your parents need the money
 c) two married sisters have to decide which of the two takes in the ageing parent
 d) your mother and father argue over whether you should leave school or go on to further education; the eventual decision goes against your own wishes
 e) you are asked to identify a shop-lifter, who is a close friend

Imagine you are in the following situations. How would you cope when:

 f) Paul was misbehaving on the school bus; but instead he finds himself accused of copying homework
 g) Sheena was expecting to be reported for poor Maths work; but instead the Head teacher tells her she is receiving a prize for English
 h) she thought she was telephoning someone from the Water Authority; but instead she finds herself talking to someone else who wanted to talk to someone from the Water Authority
 i) they had asked for egg and chips; but instead they received spaghetti
 j) he had entered hospital for therapy; but instead he found himself being taken to surgery

25

From coward to king

Two opposites confront each other: Joan, who is so strong in her self belief she appears divine; and Charles, whose reluctance to assert himself has negated all positive and outgoing qualities.

Charles from the start shows defeatism, and he is quite honest about this. He holds fast to the commonsense qualities he knows he has, as a safe rock keeping him from the leadership exposure of sailing out on his own. It is Joan's job to pull him from that rock to face the risks of the new challenge.

She does this (to change the metaphor!) by pitching back at him, like a tennis player, every response he makes, putting a new angle on each return. So eventually he has no answers left and nowhere to go but forward. Both participants, therefore, have to concentrate on each other's responses as keenly as the tennis players would. Joan serves.

Her treatment of Charles is that of the omniscient adult to the ignorant child; most importantly, however, she has to have a clear idea of the goal driving her along to provide and keep strong her motivation in the scene. Note, however, that her persuasion is not only by reason. She has a fanatical conviction of the inevitability of destiny and its divine backing, 'It's no use, Charlie, thou must face what God puts on thee!'(Line 13). Charles is eventually both beaten down and uplifted by her imperatives (trace the development of this through the text).

From coward to king

At the start of her campaign to drive the English out of France, Joan of Arc (the Maid of Orleans) has an audience with Charles, the Dauphin, to ask for command of the French army. But he is reluctant to take any part in the war.

Joan Art afraid?

Charles Yes: I am afraid. It's no use preaching to me about it . . . I only want to be left alone to enjoy myself in my own way. I never asked to be a king: it was pushed on me. So if you are going to say 'Son of St Louis: gird on the sword of your ancestors, and lead us to victory' you may spare your breath to cool your porridge; for I cannot do it. I am not built that way; and there is an end of it.

Joan Blethers! We are all like that to begin with. I shall put courage into thee.

Charles But I don't want to have courage put into me. I want to sleep in a comfortable bed . . . Put courage into the others and let them have their bellyful of fighting; but let me alone.

Joan It's no use, Charlie: thou must face what God puts on thee. If thou fail to make thyself king, thoult be a beggar: what else art fit for? Come! Let me see thee sitting on the throne. I have looked forward to that.

Charles What is the good of sitting on the throne when the other fellows give all the orders? However! *(he sits enthroned, a piteous figure)* here is the king for you! Look your fill at the poor devil.

Joan Thourt not king yet, lad: thourt but Dauphin. Be not led away by them around thee . . . I know the people: the real people that make thy bread for thee; and I tell thee they count no man king of France until the holy oil has been poured on his hair, and himself consecrated and crowned in Rheims Cathedral. And thou needs new clothes, Charlie. Why does not Queen look after thee properly?

Charles We're too poor. She wants all the money we can spare to put on her own back. Besides, I like to see her beautifully dressed; and I don't care what I wear myself; I should look ugly anyhow.

Joan There is some good in thee, Charlie; but it is not yet a king's good.

Charles We shall see. I am not such a fool as I look. I have my eyes open; and I can tell you that one good treaty is worth ten good fights. These fighting men lose all on the treaties that they gain on the fights. If we can only have a treaty, the English are sure to have the worst of it, because they are better at fighting than at thinking.

Joan If the English win, it is they that will make the treaty; and then God help poor France! Thou must fight, Charlie, whether thou will

It would be interesting to try this particular interchange as a movement exercise: Charles is now desperately trying to slither out of things, and the way she transfixes him is almost physical (Lines 7–26).

It is during this speech that Charles eventually gives in. His train of thought as he listens and finds the turning point is important (Lines 27–37).

or no . . . We must take our courage in both hands: aye, and pray for it with both hands too.

Charles Oh do stop talking about God and praying . . .

Joan Thou poor child, thou hast never prayed in thy life. I must teach thee from the beginning.

Charles I am not a child: I am a grown man and a father . . .

Joan Aye, you have a little son. He that will be Louis the Eleventh when you die. Would you not fight for him?

Charles No; a horrid boy, he hates me . . . I don't want to be bothered with children . . . I don't want to be any of these fine things that you all have your heads full of: I want to be just what I am. Why can't you mind your own business, and let me mind mine?

Joan I tell thee it is God's business we are here to do: not our own. I have a message to thee from God; and thou must listen to it, though thy heart break with the terror of it.

Charles I don't want a message; but can you tell me any secrets? Can you do any cures? . . .

Joan I can turn thee into a king, in Rheims Cathedral; and that is a miracle that will take some doing, it seems.

Charles If we go to Rheims, and have a coronation, Anne will want new dresses. We can't afford them. I am all right as I am.

Joan As you are! And what is that? Less than my father's poorest shepherd. Thou'rt not lawful owner of thy own land of France till thou be consecrated.

Charles But I shall not be lawful owner of my own land anyhow. Will the consecration pay off my mortgages? . . .

Joan Charlie: I come from the land, and have gotten my strength working on the land; and I tell thee that the land is thine to rule righteously and keep God's peace in. . . I come from God to tell thee to kneel in the cathedral and solemnly give thy kingdom to Him for ever and ever, and become the greatest king in the world as His steward and His bailiff, His soldier and His servant. The very clay of France will become holy: her soldiers will be the soldiers of God: the rebel dukes will be rebels against God; the English will fall on their knees and beg thee let them return to their lawful homes in peace. Wilt be a poor little Judas, and betray me and Him that sent me?

Charles Oh, if I only dare!

Joan I shall dare, dare, and dare again, in God's name! Art for or against me?

Charles I'll risk it. I warn you I shan't be able to keep it up; but I'll risk it. You shall see. *(Running to the main door and shouting)*. Come back everybody. *(To Joan)*. Mind you stand by and don't let me be bullied. *(Shouting again)*. Come along, will you: the whole court. *(He sits down as the members of the court enter)* Now I'm in for it; but no matter: here goes! . . . *(As the court falls silent he rises to his feet)*. . . I have given the command of the army to The Maid. The Maid is to do as she likes with it.

(Bernard Shaw: *Saint Joan*, Scene 2)

Questions/suggestions

a) and b) There are complementary qualities in Charles' character but, paradoxically, the attractive elements, instead of counter-balancing his weaknesses, seem to support them.

c) The answer to this sums up the whole of Charles' personality defect.

d) This is a relationship not unknown in the school room? Is Joan, as written, too bossy?

e) See previous notes on Joan's attitude. It is important that 'the clear idea' is kept consistently in her mind throughout the scene.

Questions/suggestions

a) How would Charles assess himself? List the main features of his character as he would see them. What would Joan's comments be on these?

b) When Joan says, 'There is some good in thee, Charlie', what aspects of his personality can she see that he might not be aware of? What extra qualities does she want to put in him when she then says, 'but it is not yet a king's good'?

c) What is Charles afraid of?

d) What attitude has Joan to Charles and how does she work on him so that he will do what she wants?

e) What is the basis of Joan's own self belief?

3 To begin with

1 This is a selection of controversial topics to stimulate interest and get the participants involved.

2 The intention of this exercise is to encourage participants to voice strong opinions within the control-structure of the interview, and so harness an approach into the drama involvement of these bridging improvisations.

3 This exercise suggests fuller improvisational situations, providing contexts for strongly defined feelings. In b) it would be preferable if the 'persuader' doesn't know he or she is disliked.

4 This provides a change of approach: an opportunity to express attitudes and feelings which are more subtle. Note that the motivation is helped by necessity (not easy to ignore) and is selflessly directed. If this exercise can be successfully managed, it should give useful practice in acceptance and sharing.

5 This section encourages the positive force needed for joint encounters played out through appropriate movement situations.

a) and b) These exercises involve types of limbering up which can extend a range of movements and prepare for closer work with other participants. Note the competitive element in each and the value of slow motion in developing the depth of movement work and aiding concentration.

c) This exercise extends the ideas of confrontation, and overcoming obstacles.

d) This exercise should be done with a partner to encourage co-operation. If possible, it should be done with someone the participant doesn't normally get on with (an assessable

measure of success if one is able to do this). As above, slow motion is both helpful and desirable. Note that 'sink to the floor, then lift each other up' can effectively be done back-to-back.

e) This exercise translates movement work into normal improvisational situations where a degree of responsibility and genuine self righteousness comes into the 'self defence'. Can the participant put his point of view rationally and without heat?

The comparison with the movement is less explicit than in Chapter 2 (*To begin with*, Exercise 2), and so more practice may be needed in matching the themes, (the spirit of the movement sequence to the events of the improvisation). Encourage the participant to devise the circumstances (the 5 'W's) of these or similar situations.

To begin with

1 Discuss the following topics:

a) the faults in present day schooling
b) the ideal state, compared with the present government
c) the reintroduction of National Service
d) the legalisation of cannabis OR banning of alcohol or tobacco
e) feminism – is it a load of rubbish?

2 Interview these people:

a) an exponent of one of the opinions in 1
b) a strike leader
c) someone currently in the news
d) a supporter of pacifism
e) an opponent of fox hunting

3 You have the following disagreements:

a) the interviewer in 2 has strongly opposing views
b) someone you dislike tries to persuade you to come to...
c) you hate dogs; a neighbour asks you to look after the dog
d) admonished for lateness, you think you are being 'picked on'
e) you are not allowed to go out after tea. Why not?

4 Give comfort or encouragement to:

a) a little creature that is lost or frightened
b) a child who is lost
c) a friend who is worried about the exams
d) someone who lost the argument
e) the supporter of a beaten team

5 Try these activities involving movement:

a) take part in a tug o' war, with an imaginary rope
b) in slow motion:
   • fight
   • fence
   • fool
   • overthrow
   • escape
c) you are confronted by a wall, a fence, a counter, a ditch. Show: the objects; how they differ; how you get through
d) with a partner:
   • move imaginary furniture from room to room
   • copy the way your partner stands, sits, walks
   • your partner takes on a particular shape, like a statue; you take on a different shape; move in and out of each other's shapes
   • sink to the floor, then lift each other
   • guide your partner, with fingers not quite touching, round a twisting route
e) devise situations where you would walk through snow, sand, a storm, a head wind, waves. Then imagine you are in situations where:
   • there is no chance to put your point of view
   • promotion to the first team is being kept from you
   • slowness is holding up production at your factory
   • police have difficulty finding the truth
   • a problem prevents acceptance of an invitation

Is this the school for us?

In this situation there is scope for an interchange or clash of opinions in coming to a decision and taking the pressure of other points of view. These may not necessarily be agreed with, but role switching gives the chance to see them objectively.

To think about

The onus of preparation is on the Head teacher. How his or her case is put and how the parents react, will sort out opinions and test their strength. The Head teacher and parents may feel constrained by the labelling of their roles. Try to avoid this.

In c), such restriction ought not to apply to the 'child', who can judge issues from the point of view of his or her own age group and whose opinion should reflect a commitment, that is, is he or she prepared to go through that form of education? This illustrates that it is not the 'right' or 'wrong' choice that matters but the participants' own attitudes and the way they are prepared to express them.

Variations

There is an opportunity for the parents to work out their views beforehand, so the task of formulating opinions now falls on the Head. However, there is still scope for change, especially when coloured by b).

In c) and d), character descriptions will need building up so that there is motivation for their use. Try mini situations to provoke this and to provide a background.

Follow-up

The follow-up is meant not only to extend the situation but also to give an opportunity for deepening, retrospectively, the opinions and methods of approach of the characters. A subsidiary effect can be the clarification of the topic itself.

Is this the school for us?

Parents visit a Head teacher about the admission of their
thirteen year old child. The school does not believe in
conventional discipline, timetables or compulsory lessons.

To think about

a) The parents wish to find out if this is the right school for their
child.
b) The Head teacher wishes to find out if the child is suitable for
admission.
c) What is the child's point of view?
d) Afterwards, will the parents still wish their child to attend that
school? Will the Head wish to accept the child?

Variations

a) The parents may already have strong views on education.
b) The parents have heard rumours that the Head:
  • is a 'con-man'
  • is a member of an extremist political or religious party
  • was sacked from his previous job
  • has been in trouble with the police
  • is about to move to another post

c) The personalities of the people involved may vary.
  • The Head teacher may be a gentle considerate man, the
    parents dogmatic bullies (and the child?).
  • The Head teacher may be supercilious and contemptuous; the
    parents may be sincerely seeking the truth.
  • They are strangers to each other and will initially be polite
    and courteous. Will this last? What might cause a change?

d) There may be differences of opinion and approach between the
husband and wife.

Follow-up

Try these situations:
a) a scene in the school
b) the Head teacher sees the parents again because of trouble with
the child
c) years later the pupil returns: to congratulate or to complain?
d) the child hates the school and says so to his parents
e) the child argues with friends who attend a different type of
school

35

And to follow

1 These are legitimate targets. That, together with the task of rationally spelling out the arguments should lead to attack and defence which are orthodox and can positively use the participant's strength of feeling, which will probably have a strong sense of justice as a base.

Can any of the topics in f)–j) be grafted into the procedure of a debate or trial? This can help to make the participants more objective and take away the negativism of, for instance, personal grievance or resentment.

2 This provides an opportunity to channel strength and energy, but also to find out what it is like to be on the receiving end of stubborn opposition. An attempt at every method of trying to get one's own way should stretch the participant. It would be useful to analyse the taxi driver's arguments and to assess who 'won' and why.

Exercises f)–j) provide further scope by the addition of extra circumstances and characters, with the participant at the centre. Note whether the participant is facing the opposition or doing the opposing. Look for opportunities to use rational argument (on both sides) instead of forcing by willpower, and see if diplomacy is needed in the face of bullying.

3 The situation can be approached in stages, for example with further investigation or action against the police. However, note the main question: is the finder innocent? Neither we nor the police should know whether he is or not.

In a)–e) note what use, if any, is made of: truth and lies; sincerity and plausibility; facts and opinions; real versus circumstantial evidence.

4 The participant is sure his opposition is important and well justified; or that is, he really believes he is right in what he is doing, what he is wearing, his hair style, etc. The challenge is to justify himself without heat or anger. He has also to be able to see the others' points of view and understand the base of their arguments. Again, role switching is desirable.

5 This is an exercise about body language and the use of objects, and an interesting by-product is to see how the 'visitor' reacts to or tries to overcome the boss's tactics. To avoid artificiality, it is important for the participants to devise and become involved in the details of the conflict situation itself, which will provide a genuine motivating base for the actions. Speech, for instance, as in the boss's replies, should occur as a natural part of the exercise of using the body in e). The body language and use of objects, in such circumstances, may occur naturally but conscious thought (and talk) about it helps to put conflict, in general, into perspective.

Situations f)–j) show that, as in life, conflict and opposition may exist in grey areas and a strong will on its own may not be enough. The exercises should help to explore 'hang-ups', if these are evident, on both sides of the barrier. Note the relevance to social and communication problems (see later chapters).

i) This exercise could include red tape, implacable authority or a family situation.

j) This can be a real situation or may have a use in a language class.

And to follow

1 Prepare the main points of a speech to attack:
  a) school rules
  b) the lack of choice in...
  c) the organisation and officials of a sport
  d) TV programming
  e) the examination system

Now prepare to defend:
  f) yourself against charges of 'loitering'
  g) your views against a political opponent
  h) a friend who is being criticised
  i) your own principles or wishes against someone who is trying to persuade you to...
  j) the justice of your case

2 A taxi is urgently needed but the only taxi driver available refuses. In order to change his mind, try these options:
  a) persuasion
  b) pleading
  c) force or threats
  d) compromise
  e) bribery

Try these other opposition situations:
  f) not being allowed to leave
  g) no entry
  h) refusal to hand something over
  i) unwillingness to tell
  j) refusal to serve

3 A handbag is found and taken to the police. It contains two hundred pounds, but it should contain twice that amount. Enact this situation, then these other accusation situations:
  a) a damaged library book
  b) paint sprayed on the wall
  c) a row in the changing rooms
  d) rowdiness on the bus
  e) cheating

4 Be as polite as you can in the following situations:
  a) a class-mate insists that favouritism is behind your high marks
  b) the teacher is sure your homework was copied
  c) if you don't change your style of dress you will lose the next five weeks' pocket money
  d) you are refused admission because of your companions
  e) someone you thought of as a friend is highly critical of your hair style and won't be seen with you

5 The boss has an unwelcome visitor (e.g. someone with a complaint). To help his or her resistance, see what use he or she can make of:
  a) the desk
  b) the visitor's chair
  c) the telephone
  d) the filing cabinets, files, and other items of equipment
  e) his or her own body (when sitting, standing, moving about)

How can the opponent overcome these barriers?

Enact situations involving other barriers:
  f) of age, sex, colour or religion
  g) when looking for a job or accommodation
  h) from someone of a different social background
  i) from the official view OR the answer, 'because I say so'
  j) when trying to make yourself understood

37

Who's boss and how?

There are two forms of strong willed behaviour shown here: the rebel attitude of Bamforth to his superiors; and the official 'hardness' of Sgt. Mitchem and Cpl. Johnstone. Motivation for Mitchem and Johnstone is the safety of the patrol (and their own safety) plus reliance on the facts of war and the army code. Bamforth is motivated by basic human feeling; perhaps more vague than the other but very necessary to provide the strength of Bamforth's commitment to his actions which, in an army context, are extreme. Any natural strength of will is useful here, and the participant can also be helped by personal feelings against Mitchem and Johnstone. You could create some reasons for Bamforth's resentment of them and play these out in mini situations.

Note that the problem in the scene is not really resolved: only 'official' violence ends it. Would this be necessarily so in real life? Try it, and possible alternative solutions, by developing the extract further through improvisation.

The implications of 'opting out', the use of violence, reliance on the 'rule book' and the morality of 'obeying orders' are also contained in the extract and are behaviourly relevant to this area.

Notice the absence of exclamation marks when Johnstone and Mitchem give orders to Bamforth. They are so secure in their authority that there is no need to shout or bluster (Lines 17 and 19).

The sub text is Mitchem recognising the significance of his action – murder – but he is matter of fact about it (Line 21).

This is the core of Mitchem's motivation (Line 23).

Here you can see Mitchem's reliance on the crutch of the rule book in order to enforce his will (Line 25).

Who's boss and how?

A British army patrol in the second world war is surrounded by Japanese in the Malayan jungle. They decide to make an attempt to break through the enemy lines. But what will they do with the Japanese prisoner who is with them?

Characters: Sgt. Mitchem, Cpl. Johnstone, L/Cpl. MacLeish, Privates Bamforth, Whitaker, Evans, Smith, and the prisoner

Johnstone . . . He's stopping where he is. *(He picks up the prisoner's bayonet from the table)* It's cobblers for him.
Bamforth No.
Mitchem I've got no choice.
Bamforth You said he was going back.
Mitchem He was – before. The circumstances altered. The situation's changed. I can't take him along.
Bamforth What's the poor get done to us?
Mitchem It's a war. It's something in a uniform and it's a different shade to mine.
Bamforth *(Positioning himself between the prisoner and Johnstone)* You're not doing it, Johnno.
Johnstone You laying odds on that?
Bamforth For Christ's sake!
Johnstone It's a bloody Nip.
Bamforth He's a man!
Johnstone Shift yourself, Bamforth. Get out of the way.
Bamforth You're not doing it.
Mitchem Bamforth, shift yourself.
Bamforth You're a bastard, Mitchem.
Mitchem I wish to God I was.
Bamforth You're a dirty bastard, Mitchem.
Mitchem As far as I'm concerned, it's all these lads or him.
Bamforth It's him or me.
Mitchem *(Crossing to join Johnstone)* Get to one side. That's an order.
Bamforth Stick it.
Mitchem For the last time, Bamforth, move over.
Bamforth Try moving me.
Mitchem I've got no time to mess about.
Bamforth So come on, Whitaker! Don't sit there, lad. Who's side you on? *(Whitaker rises slowly. For a moment it would seem he is going to stand by Bamforth but he crosses the room to stand beyond Mitchem and*

In contrast to the solidity of the others, Bamforth is now desperately threshing around for support. What would he do if it is not forthcoming? Does he know?

Notice that Cpl. Johnstone has said nothing for some time and in fact will say no more. But his mind is still working.

Meanwhile the other privates are making or have made their personal choices. It doesn't appear difficult.

'You're in it' – the 'it' means the situation, but the sub text means the guilt (Line 14).
Is Bamforth desperate here, or determined (Lines 16–17)?

Mitchem has also said nothing for some time but, like Johnstone, his mind will have been working towards the decision he now takes (Line 22).

Mitchem and Johnstone act in unison, but their communication with each other is not in words (Lines 28–29).

Johnstone) You've got no guts, Whitaker. You know that, boy. You've just got no guts.

Whitaker We've got to get back, Bammo.

Bamforth You're a gutless slob.

Whitaker I've got to get back.

Bamforth Evans. Taffy! *(Evans moves from the window)* Put the gun on these two, son.

Evans I reckon Mitch is right, you know. We couldn't get him back to camp, could we? The Nips must have a Div between the camp and us.

Bamforth He's going to kill him, you nit! . . . Smudger! Smudger, now it's up to you.

Smith Don't ask me, Bammo. Leave me out of it.

Bamforth You're in it, Smudge. You're in it up to here.

Smith I just take orders. I just do as I'm told. I just plod on.

Bamforth The plodding on has stopped. Right here. Right here you stop and make a stand. He's got a wife and kids.

Smith I've got a wife and kids myself. Drop it, Bammo, it's like Mitch says – it's him or us.

Bamforth Jock! . . . Jock! *(MacLeish continues to stare out of the window)* MacLeish! . . . *(MacLeish does not move)* . . .

Mitchem All right, Bamforth, you've had your say. Now shift.

Bamforth Shift me! Come on, heroes, shift me!

Mitchem Whitaker! Grab a gun and cover the Nip.

Bamforth Don't do it, Whitaker. Stay out of it.

Mitchem Whitaker!

(Whitaker picks up a sten from the table and crosses to cover the prisoner who has realised the implications and is trembling with fear. Mitchem and Johnston move in to overpower Bamforth . . .)

(Willis Hall: *The Long and the Short and the Tall*, Act 2)

Questions/suggestions

a) Here the participants will need to look into themselves and explore their own motives and attitudes to what is in fact a crucial decision.

b) Further exploration of motive is needed here but it is also necessary to look for 'another way'.

c) Role-switching might help to answer the question, that is, in what characters do the participants feel most comfortable in action? The implication relates to qualities of personality (but not necessarily to 'right' or 'wrong' ones).

d) Ask them.

e) The prisoner knows no English. Therefore, to understand the scene, the person playing him must try and wash out all he hears, and look for evidence in tone of voice, action, body language and other visual signs. This is also a challenge to the other players. As an experiment, try the scene in movement alone or in an 'assumed language'.

Questions/suggestions

a) Which character do you identify with most easily? Why?

b) Justify the motives of Mitchem, Johnstone and Bamforth. Try out the situation as one of rational argument rather than one of confrontation.

c) Johnstone and Mitchem are figures of authority because of their rank. Imagine they did not have that rank: would it make any difference to the way they behave? Suppose Bamforth was the sergeant? Would he behave any differently (from them or from his normal behaviour)?

d) What would be Bamforth's opinions of the other characters and how might this affect the way he makes a stand? Why do Whitaker, Evans, Smith and MacLeish not join with him in this stand?

e) If you were the prisoner, what would you be thinking of the other men's actions and behaviour? Would you try any intervention yourself?

4 To begin with

1 This starts with a very basic concentration exercise using memory and observation to focus the mind. It is harder than it appears and will benefit from practice. It is literal at first, then, in f)–j), uses the imagination (and opens up words and action) but keeps the focus tight.

2 The introduction of a partner for pair work is another aspect and test of co-ordination. At first, the physical co-ordination of leading and following is required, but the suggestions in brackets give an opportunity to involve feelings and attitudes. Music is also relevant here (see notes to 3 and 5). Note that in hand leading, the forefingers of each partner should be barely touching (less than a centimetre apart) and it is a relevant task to maintain that distance during the movement.

3 This exercise involves specific movements based on something familiar. As with all movement work, look for fullness and the whole use of the body (i.e. more than just use of the arms). Take the time to build up concentration and let the imagination grow and form a context. The movement and the imagination and concentration can be helped by use of slow motion, enlargement or a time schedule for each action (structured with a beginning, middle and end). For variation, introduce different situations, for example on a windy day, when tired etc., and, for stylisation, use music and/or rhythmic backgrounds. Note that the music can be more than an accompaniment or match: it can suggest, stimulate and help create further and more varied movement.

4 This is an introduction to the idea of location, which in itself is indicating and giving the experience of form and pattern, and is further developed through action. Different locations might be suggested by the participants, and all can be used as a base for other actions

and characters, moving into the co-ordination necessary to organise and attempt situations and stories.

Note that e) refers to real furniture etc.

5 Co-ordination of actions with a partner also develops an individual's ability in movement. These exercises can take an extended time to develop and a lot of grafting to add detail. With practice and greater confidence, the participants will 'follow' each other for longer periods as they sustain the concentration; then there will be greater scope for development of their own ideas and further development to freer, more personally imaginative movement.

Note the previous references (in 2 and 3) to slow motion, enlargement (imagine, for instance, being a giant while doing the action), a time schedule, rhythm accompaniment (e.g. a drum, counting and handclapping, all of which can vary in intensity) and, of course, music. Here we are on the threshold of dance-drama where music can make the following contributions:

- it helps relaxation and can awaken activity
- it induces a mood or suggests an atmosphere
- it is a stimulus to ideas and story
- it can generate or heighten feelings and attitudes
- it matches shape of movement, but also stimulates and creates it

In general, the framework of a musical beat and the shape of its tune provide both a structured frame for and a creative guide to personal expressive bodily development, which has its own less obvious co-ordinated structure.

To begin with

1 Look out of the window and concentrate on all you can see. Turn around and describe what you saw. Then do the same with:
- a) a tray of objects
- b) a picture
- c) what someone is wearing
- d) a pattern or design
- e) furnishings and fittings

Use as much detail as you can in these situations:
- f) check the contents of a drawer (imaginary)
- g) fill a backpack (also imaginary) for a camping holiday
- h) list all the equipment needed for a particular hobby
- i) explain (on the telephone) to a stranger how you can be recognised
- j) imagine you are listening to a lecture on road safety; repeat four of the main points made

❖

2 Lead a partner, first with eye contact then with forefingers along:
- a) a swamp (why is he frightened?)
- b) a track through the bushes (looking for what?)
- c) a bombed building (where are you going?)
- d) an underground cave (when will she be found?)
- e) the girders (who is chasing you?)

❖

3 Try these different actions:
- a) polishing a window
- b) painting a door
- c) folding sheets
- d) raking a seed bed
- e) hanging out clothes
- f) saving a penalty
- g) taking a catch

- h) strokes in tennis
- i) a touch-down
- j) heading away

❖

4
- a) Imagine the ground floor of your house and show someone round, describing each room as you do so.
- b) Show how you would:
  - boil an egg in the kitchen
  - fit a new plug in the living room
  - hang curtains in the bedroom
  - mop up in the bathroom
  - lay the table in the dining room
- c) Set out a garden.
- d) Imagine an area which can include some activity (e.g. a garage, a gym). It gets larger, then gets smaller. Adapt your activity each time.
- e) Arrange furniture and other items in the room to suggest:
  - a bus
  - an office
  - fortifications
  - a ship
  - a work shop

❖

5 As if looking in a mirror, face or follow a partner to match his or her shapes and movements. Then make contrasting shapes and movements, filling in the space your partner creates. Try these examples:
- a) jobs in the house and garden (note the shapes made by actions in 3)
- b) letters of the alphabet and hands of the clock
- c) animal shapes and movements
- d) walking on different surfaces, for example ice, snow, mud etc.
- e) statues, in shape and motion

45

What's in store?

Setting the scene

In this exercise concentration should be on the details of the location, and the activity within it, to keep the focus tight. Note that real objects (e.g. desks, tables or boxes) can be used, but imaginary ones are just as effective once the participant gets used to mini locations within the main locations, and to general positioning (e.g. the door staying in the same place, or the height of the counter staying constant). This is also a useful control factor.

Setting the characters

Be prepared to spend time building up truth and reality in the people rather than rushing into quick 'characters'. Mini exercises on how the characters relate to each other and to situations (e.g. within the shop, buying and selling generally or customer conversations) will help to answer the questions posed and the resulting detail should heighten believability in the participants.

What happens?

In addition you can use any story or situation the participants suggest, especially any that arise from 'leading remarks'. Doing this section is usually slow and steady and progress will be revealed in:

a)   the participants' own invention of detail and incidents and their ability to organise and develop these

b)   acceptance of the reality and location of each situation as natural circumstances in which they feel at ease

c)   believable behaviour in the situation, showing involvement in action, character and relationships

What's in store?

This is a situation in a shop. The plot, to begin with, is not important. What is important is the reality and detail of the scene itself, so that one action can logically lead to another.

Setting the scene

a) Try the following exercises:
- when opening a door, show the difference between going out and coming in
- when watching TV, indicate a large room, then a small room
- when looking for something, show the difference between an attic and a cellar

b) Establish what type of shop it is. If possible relate the shop to your hobby or interests.

c) Set the shop out as a location. Decide where the shelves, door, counter, windows etc. are situated.

d) Devise appropriate activities to take place in the shop, for example:
- setting out a window display
- ordering goods on the telephone
- explaining how to use goods (e.g. D.I.Y. tools) to a customer
- showing the shop is crowded, empty, busy, noisy, hot

Setting the characters

You can build up the characters in simple buying or selling situations:

a) The boss: what sort of person is she or he, what sort of background does he or she come from? Could you easily be that sort of person? If not, how would you change?

b) The assistants: they can be as varied as people normally are. Are they keen or are they bored? Are they experienced or are they just starting? How do they get on with the boss?

c) The customers: they can be similarly varied. How do they treat the boss, his assistants and each other?

What happens

Try these situations:

a) customer situations, for example a customer is short-changed (is it a genuine mistake or not?), queries, complaints, arguments

b) crime situations, for example a shop-lifter, a raid, a bomb scare

c) boss and assistant situations, for example rebellion, wrongful accusation

d) problem situations, for example competition, rivalry, threat of closure

47

And to follow

1 The structuring of the previous section should be useful here for ideas, plot and character development. Participants should be encouraged to suggest other locations.

2 The main challenge here is for the partner, who has the task of concentrated listening in order to spot the detail. If there is a 'real' story behind the 'tall' one, this can be enacted.

Exercises f)–j) show interplay of attitudes, thoughts and feelings, with variations suggested by different locations and people. Can the participants involve themselves in the argument sufficiently for these variations to arise naturally and appropriate interplay to develop?

3 This section deals with the skill in relating to someone by telephone; then the contrast of a face-to-face encounter. Variation should also occur as a result of differing relationships. Even though it is only at an introductory level there is scope for (and the effort of) a new thought and attitude in each exercise (see also Chapter 6).

4 This involves group co-ordination, which should be assisted by the formal framework. Emphasis is placed on the role of the chairperson and on the ability to co-ordinate (or sense the feeling of co-ordination) and to work for unity. Topics may actually be real (e.g. a class magazine) as well as imaginary, and they involve the skills of discussion. Wider variations of this framework are also exemplified (with a different objective) in Chapter 7 (*And to follow* – Exercise 3).

5 In a)–c) the situation is tightly controlled by its built-in factors, whose detail should, as the situation progresses, help to develop a closely focused and concentrated involvement. From this secure base the participant then moves out into the freer opportunities of d)–e). Is the transition undertaken as a natural development? If not, go back for a more 'imposed' activity and/or build control factors into d)–e).

Exercises f)–j) should illustrate the co-ordination required to be part of the structure of a story. As above, there is a basis for later more individual work. Variation can be introduced with other sequences, locations and occasions.

And to follow

1 Try out these scenes and locations:

a) a queue at the police station
b) waiting at the altar
c) mistaken identity at the dentist's
d) a quarrel at the disco
e) fun at the fair
f) mystery over the wall
g) a lucky find – on deck or at the beach
h) a guard on the fence
i) an accident: in the kitchen; in the woods; in the changing room; at the factory; on duty

2 While you are telling a 'tall story' your partner has to try and break it down. Try these examples:
a) a fishing trip that broke records
b) a night out that got into the papers
c) your brother's incredible job
d) a fabulous holiday
e) your fantastic present

Imagine that you are having an argument over the statement 'We can't afford it', in the following situations:
f) in the house
g) out in the street
h) inside the shop
i) joined by a friend
j) faced by the waiter (or shop assistant)

3 Ring up a garden centre to order plants and imagine that:
a) you want a favour
b) the person at the other end seems very stupid
c) you are suspicious of something
d) you recognise the voice of a friend whom you have not seen for two years
e) you recognise the voice of someone you have had a fight with

Now try these situations again, this time when visiting the garden centre.

4 You are having a discussion with a group of people. Although not everyone agrees, someone has to guide the group to a conclusion about:
a) what goes in the magazine (editorial board)
b) where to go on holiday (family)
c) how to improve the village (local council or local society)
d) who does what in the concert (group)
e) how to market a new cosmetic (sales team)

5 Try these situations in space:

a) Carry out a full investigation of the space craft, inside and out. One person should explain the controls to the others
b) Arrange yourselves inside the craft; what jobs are to be done?
c) You are in flight– report back to ground control
d) You are on a strange planet; move to and from the space craft. Meeting with a strange creature, you find out about each other. How?
e) Develop one of the situations further.

Now imagine these situations in war time:
f) a farmer finds someone sleeping in a barn – a foreigner
g) this person persuades the farmer that he is an Allied escaped p.o.w., but he is really a spy
h) he asks the farmer to help him escape to his own country
i) the farmer introduces him to the resistance network
j) the spy is unmasked, and...

49

Windy boy in a windswept tree

This poem was chosen because of the way in which it brings together, within the framework of a sequence, physical movement and a mental state which can encompass a range of feelings (e.g. excitement, fear, panic, relief).

It can be read aloud as an accompaniment and background for a unit of movement work which combines the physical and the emotional. Although it is an exercise for an individual, a whole group can do it at once; all members taking part (and of course it needn't be only a 'boy' who is up the tree!).

No special apparatus is necessary, a chair or a bench being quite adequate; although if a genuine tree is available, try it! Although athleticism is an asset it is not necessarily the criterion for success in the activity. The outcome to look for is how convincingly the participant interprets his or her relationship, through the use of the body, with the object (the 'tree') and how far the participant's emotional involvement in the situation expresses itself imaginatively through the movements (perhaps just in the face?). There can be as many interpretations as there are members in the group.

Windy boy in a windswept tree

The branch swayed. swerved,
Swept and whipped up,
Down, right to left,
Then leapt to the right again,
As if to hurl him down
To smash to smithereens
On the knife-edge grass
Or smother
In the close-knit quilts of moss.
Out on a crazy limb
He screwed his eyes tight shut,
To keep out the dizzy ground.
Sweat greased his palms:
Fear pricked his forehead.
The twisted branches lunged and lurched,
His body curved, twisted, he arched
His legs and gripped the bark
Between his ankles.
The crust of the bark
Sharp as glasspaper
And rough with wrinkles
Grazed his skin
And raised the raw red flesh
And crazed his mind
With fear of breaking.
then the mad-cap, capering wind
Dropped.
The branch steadied,
Paused,
Rested.
He slowly clambered, slowly, back,
Slowly, so safely,
Then dropped
Like a wet blanket
To rock-like, reassuring ground.
Finally, without a sound,
He walked carefully
Home.

(Geoffrey Summerfield)

Questions/suggestions

a) Many exercises would be suitable for limbering up. This particular one takes another angle on the poem: one which follows its spirit and should be valuable for later movement work.

b) This is a way of breaking down the interpretation by the simple relationship of movement to the feelings behind it.

c) If all three of these foci can be brought together it will be a culmination not only of the poem but of the participant's own involvement and efforts.

d) Relief has been mentioned, but how relevant is a consideration of anticlimax (as opposed to declimax), and what emotion underlies the almost imposed silence?

e) Speech and language, previously absent, seem a natural conclusion. An exercise around the poem would be that of translating the experience into a pattern and sequence of sound (see also *To begin with* in Chapter 7).

Questions/suggestions

a) The first four lines describe the movement of the branch. Try to move as if you were that branch.

b) What are the feelings of the boy in the storm? How do his actions show these feelings? Try out the actions on a beam or a chair.

c) The ending of the poem is calm and peaceful. Describe and try out the stages of movement that lead to that ending in:
  • the wind
  • the branch
  • the boy

d) What are the boy's thoughts as he walks home? Why is it 'without a sound'?

e) When you return home, tell your story to someone.

4a   Special needs supplement

1 The objective in these exercises is to introduce the participants to basic space awareness through movement which requires personal control and variation and in a progression involving shape and pattern (as a co-ordinating base).

When working on the exercises, sound and language may break in and obviously are to be encouraged. However, in both 1 and 2, one can actively promote this development, especially if the movement situations are related to contexts: for example movements involving stretching or pulling could turn into rescue or escape situations, beckoning movements could become a cry for help, and so on. Follow ups to such situations could involve further language through telling the story to the family, the press, the police, etc.

2 Contact exercises have a clear connection with co-ordination, as well as communication, relationships and identification, and they have more than a physical benefit. They are simply done as pair work (all members of the group working at once) and gain from an extended slow motion approach (note the reference to 'large' shapes) and from repeated practice. Other suggestions for shapes, which might be given by the group, should help this.

b) This exercise should benefit the 'guider' as well as those navigating the 'routes' because of the demands made with concentrating and forming and remembering a pattern in the mind.

c) The 'magnetism' of specific objects (e.g. a light bulb) is a convenient way of helping participants to rise and fall and become aware of the use of

1

a) Bounce an imaginary ball around the room. After a while:
  i)   the ball gets bigger and bigger
  ii) the ball gets smaller and smaller
  iii) there are parts of the floor you and the ball must avoid
  iv) as you go over the floor, try and make recognisable shapes in your movements (e.g. a triangle or a figure 8); then repeat them several times
  v)   with a partner, work out actions you can do with this imaginary ball

b) Clip an imaginary hedge with a pair of shears. Tackle it from all angles. Then start cutting out shapes (e.g. of birds or flowers). Afterwards, get rid of the clippings.

c) Pick up imaginary pins scattered all over the floor. Then make a pattern on the floor with them. Walk around the shape of this pattern. It gets bigger and bigger.

d) Break out of an imaginary:
  i)   paper bag
  ii) dustbin
  iii) chain
  iv) seat belt and then car
  v)   cupboard

e) Start by making skipping movements and then turn them into movements from skating, football, tennis, badminton and basketball.

2

a) Follow, with your eyes only, as a partner draws in the air with his finger the large shape of:
  i)   a letter of the alphabet
  ii) a number
  iii) an animal
  iv) a flower
  v)   an item of furniture

b) Across the room, guide a partner with your eyes to:
  i)   come towards you
  ii) move from spot to spot
  iii) reach up, down, across; then bend and sway

levels and heights. Once work has been done on elbow-to-elbow, other parts of the body can be used. Note that the actions here are done together but need one person to lead. First one partner should do this, then the other.

d) The use of statues and sculpturing is helpful to develop an awareness of shape and to maintain posture. Some examples are given here but others may spring to mind and can include abstract shapes, where the test is to 'justify' the shape chosen (e.g. why are you stretching? where are you?). This provides motivation and a context. A follow-up activity could bring the statues to life in action (and also in context); first in slow motion, then at normal speed, then to the speed, rhythm, shape and intensity of a sound accompaniment or music (see earlier exercises in this chapter).

e) This exercise deals specifically with music and the obvious development is to bring in real instrumentation, even in a simple form. Allow imagination to be used at first, however.

Rhythm and dance can be used to develop co-ordination in v) which is a simplified version of the *To begin with* exercise v). You can build towards that level if the participants make sufficient progress.

3 These exercises use foundations of drama involvement as a base for more imaginative movement work. There is scope in b) and c) for group work, but within these sequences the action can still be interpreted at an individual level if anyone is not ready for fuller, more co-ordinated activity.

The exercises can be developed further by translating them into fuller drama sequences, matching the movement sequences already undergone. It may be necessary to help with suggestions. These might include:

- an old person reminiscing
- a spy (or spies) searching and interrupted by...
- situations involving: soldiers on duty; sport; dancing; concerts; a fete or carnival
- situations to show: grace and strength, rising and falling, growth and development, by people who have these qualities
- warmth from a friendly person, heat from anger

Note that with d) there is a time sequence of development, which may require some sort of commentary or signalling from a central figure such as the teacher or group leader.

iv) move along in a random line, anywhere over the room
v) move along a planned line (e.g. the shape of a triangle, or from door to window via the radiator)

c) Imagine your right elbow is a magnet, attracted to different objects in the room; then contact the left elbow of a partner to:
i) complete a circle
ii) stretch from side to side
iii) sink to the ground
iv) rise up again
v) lead out of the room

d) Shape yourself, then shape a partner, into the following statue shapes:
i) a boxer
ii) a runner breasting the tape
iii) a creature from outer space
iv) someone searching
v) someone sheltering

e) Hum the tune of a song. Then:
i) tap it out with your fingers, then your feet
ii) play it on a set of imaginary drums or other instruments
iii) beat out the rhythm with hand clapping
iv) make up movements to match the pattern of the music
v) do iv) while facing a partner, where one matches the movements of the other

3

a) Put yourself into the shape of a grandfather clock as it stands at one end of the room. Make the sounds and the actions of the clock. What does the clock see as it stands there? It does nothing, but later it can remember and tell all that it saw.

b) At night, the rats emerge to search for food among the tables and chairs; sometimes they think they hear noises; sometimes they help each other; sometimes they are rivals. Then a huge cat enters the room. What happens next?

c) After midnight, the toys come to life: the soldiers march and drill; the dolls dance; the cars race; the balls bounce; and so on. Who are you?

d) The layers of a bulb are tightly curled together, but slowly unfold to become leaves and a flower; after flourishing and growing in the warmth of the sun, the plant fades and droops as colder weather comes. Can you become that bulb?

57

4 The emphasis in this exercise should be on detail, as it is easy to miss out the minutiae. Some detail may seem unimportant, but it is the noticing and recording that is important. You can expect some gaps in commentary in the initial stages: it takes time to get sufficient concentration to 'keep up' with what is going on. A variation would be to commentate on what is going on generally, for example to describe what is seen from the window to the others who are not looking.

Exercises f)–j) are in a progression, to bring in the imagination. If they are done successfully they will probably be an indication of similar success in the base exercises of a)–e).

Try, if possible, to feed in variations of context to give depth and motivation to the imagined scenes, for example suppose the 'peculiar man' is being viewed from inside a hairdresser's shop, and he then enters it?

Also, for further variation, try to do the visualised scenes in action.

5 The telephone provides an element of structure, its conventions and distancing give a framework for organising communication. The emphasis in a)–e) is on doing this step by step, with one level cleared before the next is taken up. The exercise includes elements of social skills and social development, with some use of the imagination, voice range and, in e), personal motivation.

Examples f)–j) build on the base to give an opportunity for personal involvement in the relationships of a situation and more scope, even at this simple level, for individual initiative and invention.

An obvious development is to try some of these exchanges on a face to face basis to see if and how they differ. It would be interesting to see if any of the participants find this more difficult because they are not able to 'hide' behind a telephone.

e) A flame can flicker and dance and shoot out sparks as it gives warmth and cheer; but the same flames can harm and destroy. Can you be all these different flames?

4

Describe exactly all details of a set of actions as they are done by other members of the group. Examples could be:

a) playing head tennis
b) stacking chairs
c) arm wrestling
d) searching for something hidden
e) arranging objects

Give a similar commentary on an imagined scene, as if you could actually see it happening. Examples could be:

f) someone mending a roof
g) a hold-up
h) a race
i) a peculiar man in the street
j) a rescue

5

You are talking to a friend on the telephone. Imagine that:

a) your friend gives you instructions on how to get to his or her home for a party

b) you ring another friend to pass on these directions. It is a bad line

c) you are disconnected. Ring again. It is a wrong number. Try once more

d) you carry on the conversation. This time it is a better line

e) your friend is not keen to go to the party. Try persuading him or her

6 These are simple conversations, but not necessarily easy. They demand interaction or decision making and, in some cases, conflict or argument. However, that very demand can be a stimulus to start the conversation and the interaction can lead to its development. Merely getting the conversation 'off the ground' is a measure of success in this area, and if a resolution or decision is achieved then we are moving into improvisation proper and approaching a drama situation. As is so often the case in this type of progress, depth and motivation can be given by feeding in details, especially of the 5 'W's, for example in a), why are you 'in a hurry'?; in c), who is the 'stranger' and what might be his effect?

The process of transforming the conversation is given an extra dimension in f)–j) by a freer use of the imagination.

7 The more formal framework of the interview is a further step towards the development of organisation within co-ordination. It differs from the other modes of conversation in being a prescribed unit with a beginning, a middle and an end. It ought to have a built-in plan of progress, relevant, carefully thought out questions (with a closely defined purpose in their wording) and a specific function or motive (to find out what?) from the interviewer.

The three sections in this exercise are intended to show the graded progress of this organisation: a)–e) give a selection of questions for adhering to a fixed programme; f)–j) open up the scope of enquiry with the opportunity

Now try these telephone conversations:

f) a friend who was absent that day rings up to ask what you did at school

g) while making plans for a holiday you wish to change some of your companion's ideas

h) the date and time of the match has been changed; make new arrangements to go with your friend

i) you ask to have your TV repaired. Explain what is wrong and how to get to your house

j) a salesman is selling video equipment and tries to persuade you to see him

6

You are talking to the following people. What do you say when:

a) the old lady is asking questions, but you are in a hurry
b) you think you spent the money well, but your mother doesn't agree
c) meeting a stranger
d) two people hear a noise upstairs
e) rain has washed out the trip. What else can you do?

Now try conversations between these different objects:

f) toys talk about their owners
g) two vacuum cleaners describe the rooms they have cleaned
h) inside the fridge; who will be most in demand?
i) what the TV sets think of their viewers
j) the clocks compare their previous homes

7

Select five questions you could use if you were interviewing the person below. Then do the interview.

a) a record breaking athlete
b) a football manager
c) a pop star
d) someone you have seen on a television programme
e) the monarch, or any member of the royal family

for a freer range of questions, but still keeping a tight focus on the target; k)–o) are now completely free for the interviewer to construct his own programme and organise it.

The important test is whether the participant shows a similar pattern of progress.

8 In this exercise we try to put a group sequence together, step by step and building from elements in previous exercises (e.g. try interviewing the head cook). The teacher or group leader might need to play a more participatory part in sharing ideas, helping with suggestions and organisation, maybe taking a role and guiding the development of the story. This suggestion is perhaps suitable for the younger age group (see 9 for an exercise suitable for older age groups).

9 This exercise is all about structuring. The stages a)–e) give an appreciation, as the participants do it, of how a plot can be built up (and how the participants' own involvement is also built up). Stages f)–j) are left open-ended to provide the challenge for their own creative development, with help on ideas and suggestions if it is needed.

Note that from an organisational angle, a)–e) are largely exercises for an individual working with others, whereas f)–j) are more genuine group exercises.

One person should pretend to be someone well known. By asking questions, see if you can guess:

f) who it is
g) where that person has been
h) what that person has done
i) the person's occupation
j) the person's likes and dislikes

Try out these interviews:

k) an old man who has led an exciting life
l) a school-leaver who has started a new job
m) a shopkeeper who is fed-up
n) a local police officer
o) a cartoon character

8

You are to make a pie:

a) do the individual actions, for example cutting up the meat, slicing the onions, rolling out the pastry, measuring the ingredients

b) members of the group should work on particular jobs; instructions are given by the head cook

c) describe where the kitchen is and for whom the pie is being made. What might be the next stage?

d) enact a situation based on a pie being made for an important visitor, when something unexpected occurs

e) work out and do a story beginning '...The King has lost his appetite and the town crier has been instructed to search for a special cook who can cure him

9

a) Open up the shoe-shop in the morning and check that everything is in its place. Make a cup of coffee.

b) Your first customer arrives: a mother with her daughter. They try on shoes, buy a pair and depart.

c) During the morning other customers call, with differing requirements. They are attended to.

10 This is a final practice in open-ended situations or stories containing challenges and demands and requiring further development. How far are the participants now able to 'get together' both themselves and the previous drama elements they have worked on? Deductions from earlier exercises should fall naturally into the action but, in particular, you might look at what has been absorbed about:

- participating with involvement and identification
- the use of detail
- the use of the imagination
- co-ordinated contact with people and locations
- the ability to structure

d) It is lunch time. Lock up the shop and go for lunch. On your return, you notice that the door is open. You enter and see a thief escaping. You try and follow but the thief gets away.

e) Phone the police. Describe the incident and give an eye witness description. The police call to check what is missing, take photographs and finger-prints.

Here are some other ways in which the situation might be developed further:

f) police think they know the thief
g) you yourself thought you recognised him as...
h) later that night you meet him again
i) the thief left something behind
j) there is an identity parade and a case of mistaken identity

10

a) A son comes home with a torn jacket; his mother wants to know what it is all about. Does she then take action?

b) In a cafe you lay the table and serve a customer. He tries to leave without paying.

c) Jen, Jo and Harry are involved in:
- a trip to the zoo
- discovering a locked door
- collecting a reward

During the situation they become Bossy Jen, Sulky Jo and Happy Harry.

d) A relation is coming to stay for a few nights. You are asked to move out of your room. You suggest another arrangement...

e) The car won't start. A passing motorist helps to fix it, then drives away, but leaves behind a jacket, containing a lot of money.

The lawn mower

From a drama point of view, the poem provides a framework for concentration on detail and action, the second following on from the first, but also influenced by it. Following a reading the participants should take in to their activity the precise visual sharpness of the observation and the active effect that comes from the nature of the imagery.

The poem is worked on and absorbed and then becomes a background (read aloud) for the action.

Questions/suggestions

a) This is a simple basic movement. The experience of the poem is a creative stimulus for extra, varied action in addition to its function of being a model for exemplification.

b) Note the use of detail for concentration and memory, and for staying in the atmosphere and ambience of the situation.

c) This is a follow-up activity, hoping to maintain the impetus.

d) Similarly, this is follow-up work, but this time adding variety and enlargement, with scope for imaginative invention.

e) This takes the invention one stage further by introducing the relationship to other people, with the purpose of identifying. From that, there can be further participation in action and the creation or organisation of situations.

The lawn mower

With a sudden jerk, I push.
The shining stainless blades scythe the grass
And bite into the dandelion stalks
Where white juices ooze out creating a milky mass.

Brittle twigs splinter.
Hairy moss and grass are hurled in arcs,
Gather in piles
And shuffle softly in the enamel tin.

A soft whirr is heard.
The blades catch on some couch grass.
Then with a sudden jerk it runs smoothly on
Leaving behind a shaven carpet.

(June Thomson)

Questions/suggestions

a) Push an imaginary lawn mower to try out the action of this
   poem. Note:
   • how you start
   • when you push smoothly
   • when you don't, and why

b) By hand, empty the imaginary contents of the 'enamel tin' on to
   a compost heap. Look back over the lawn and notice where the
   different items came from.

c) Carry on mowing after you have heard the poem read aloud.
   How does the mower deal with the rest of the lawn? What else
   goes into the tin?

d) Make a list of other articles that are used for cutting. Put each
   one into a situation and use it. Can the situation turn into a
   story?

e) Can you think of a person to match each article? What sort of
   person? What situations might that person find himself or
   herself in? What actions might the person use?

67

5 To begin with

1 The initial concentration and memory work provide a base for imaginative involvement, with an overall emphasis on the senses; hence, when lying down, what is seen, heard, felt, smelt through the imagination with eyes closed, is very important. The descriptions are also an exercise in oral composition and communication and, as with all the accounts in this section, can be given out individually or to the group as a whole. If accounts are vague and skimpy, probe them to bring out more detail, and sharpen up any day-dreaming.

Try to find a bridge between the imagined visualisation and the imagined participation: for example a washover of water removes the first picture to leave a blank; then, as if on a photographic plate, the second picture slowly comes through.

2 Communication becomes more specifically directed in this exercise and is given a context in the emotions, springing often from a need. The notion of a 'need' illustrates the general importance of a trigger. One doesn't really 'feel' feelings (one feels an emotional reaction towards or about the thing that is causing the feelings) and so there is a need for some definite fact, occurrence, etc. to spark feelings off. Both partners benefit from this exercise, because the emotions involved affect each person.

Some sort of distancing can be useful if involvement is at first found difficult. Hence the suggestion about the telephone which helps concentration and makes it easier (less confrontational) for those who may be a little inhibited.

Note that in e) it is desirable that the listener is not aware beforehand which is the true version.

3 The intention in this exercise is for real happenings to be recounted. If they have not been experienced, questioning and conversation might draw out similar ones or prompt a similar mood. This exercise can provide a base for later imaginative involvement in the improvisational experience of the feelings.

4 The subjects of these interviews have been selected for their imaginative appeal, hence the 'romantic' or empathy aspect of history. You could also use characters from fiction. The stimulus should be curiosity. These can go down well as a group interview.

5 Again, a real happening is called for, and the intention is deliberately analytical, to help understanding and awareness of attitudes, feelings and states of mind that have been personally experienced in the past. This means remembering 'how you felt'. This can also be a help for future projection, where the attitudes, etc. will be imagined and 'triggers' will be needed, but even an awareness that such areas exist can be a mark of achievement.

Note that the contexts would normally be done separately. With familiarity, however, there could be material and scope here for some sort of sequence or story (maybe as an exercise in imaginative projection).

To begin with

1 Try to recollect everything you would normally see when standing outside your house. Describe this to the rest of the group. Then imagine it a hundred years ago, or a hundred years hence.

Now lie on the floor, with your eyes closed. Imagine you are lying on a beach under a hot sun. Concentrate on all that would be around you. Then imagine yourself taking some part in the scene. Describe the scene and your part in it. Do the same for these other scenes:
 a) a storm against the cliffs
 b) rain on the street corner
 c) excitement on the field
 d) darkness in the forest
 e) extreme cold at the cross roads

2 You are having these conversations with a partner (they can be on the telephone):
 a) you are going on holiday with a friend; your friend wants to back out; try and persuade him or her not to
 b) a reward is given for finding a necklace; the recipient was expecting more
 c) you give reasons why you can't or won't do extra work (or a particular job)
 d) your parent wishes you to wear a particular item of clothing to a party. You hate it
 e) you correct someone else's story and give your own (true?) version
 f) you tell a friend why he or she needn't be afraid of...
 g) you explain to an old person how to jump from a swing
 h) you give an account of your trip to someone who wished he or she had gone
 i) you elaborate to a friend why he or she shouldn't dislike...
 j) you describe what you would like to receive, and give, at Christmas

3 Describe the details of, and how you felt about:
 a) a new baby in the family
 b) a vital win
 c) your first trip to...
 d) the narrow escape
 e) the unexpected visitor

4 Try these interviews:
 a) your ideal house
 b) yourself – today, and in ten years time
 c) who you would like to be
 d) a Martian's view of your country
 e) a ghost
 f) a traveller on one of the first railways
 g) a survivor from...?
 h) one of Columbus' crew
 i) a Victorian servant
 j) your grandparents talking about their childhood

5 Describe to a partner a memory which involves:
 a) regret
 b) satisfaction
 c) sadness
 d) disillusion
 e) anticipation
 f) joy
 g) fear
 h) disappointment
 i) curiosity
 j) distaste

69

Is it a bomb?

Examples of the *Mr Men* books might be a useful introduction for those who may not have seen the series. However, the idea is as old as literature itself. The gender limitation is of course a convenient label; it could just as easily be Mrs or Miss, etc.

To think about

Can we make them more than mere Mr Men? That is the challenge, because the danger is that the character becomes a stereotype. It is important therefore that the characters are realistically motivated (as in a), are capable of variety (as in b), are understood by their relationship to the participant's own personality (as in c) and contain fullness, depth and detail (as in d).

Supporting activity

This exercise continues to build up realism through an exposure to a variety of detail and the use of other contexts. The characters in the main situation may need some initial opportunity to show their personality, so if these supportive exercises are worked through in some detail they can be the groundwork for genuine involvement (i.e. the participant sees himself *as* that person).

Allied with the objective of naturalness in the action is the ability to see the characteristics in relation to one's own normal conduct. So, stop the action should it appear false, and challenge the reality of the behaviour, comparing it, for instance, with the participant's own behaviour: 'Would *you* act in that way if you were certain, careful, nervous, unsure, etc?'

Follow-up

This development from what has gone before can only succeed if the non-stereotyping base is now in place. A variation of contexts is now needed. For example, devise extra situations for Mr Unsure to show and practise his improvements. These could be during an auction sale, at a travel agent's, in the market, as an attendant, explaining the rules of a game; any situation requiring decisiveness.

Is it a bomb?

Invent characters whose names reflect their main characteristic as was done in the *Mr Men* books by Roger Hargreaves. For example, Mr Certain and Mrs Unsure are shopping in a crowded store. They find a parcel. It could be suspicious.

To think about

a) The reason behind the characteristic. Why is Mr Certain certain? Is it because he knows his subject so well? Or because he can't see another point of view? These inner reasons are more important than outward signs, but they do lead to them, as in b).

b) The type of characteristic. Mr Certain's certainty can be shown by someone who is quiet but decisive and definite or someone who is ignorant, dogmatic and loud. Both may be right, or wrong.

c) How far you may need to add to or take away from your own personality in order to become the character

d) Other methods of building up the character: for example working out a life history and background

Supporting activity

a) A simple exchange of views: for example, Mr Certain is accused of a mistake or is asked his opinion on some controversial topic

b) Physical action: for example Miss Awkward and Miss Careful are engaged in some dometic activity

c) A setting: for example, how and why might Mr Unsure behave in a bus station, a doctor's surgery or a check-out

d) Other people: for example, suppose Mrs Nervous becomes embroiled with a ticket collector, the boss or a caller at the front door

Follow-up

A person's characteristics may change during a situation and, if he has weaknesses, he may improve. For example Mr Unsure could become more decisive. This can be helped if Mr Unsure works on:

a) knowing his facts more accurately

b) having a higher opinion of himself

c) taking a greater interest in other people in the situation

d) helping someone worse off than himself

e) practising situations requiring decisiveness

71

And to follow

1 The objectives here are:

- to increase the familiarity with aspects of character: for example moods, feelings, etc., for the participant's personal enrichment
- to strengthen the idea of motivation
- to reinforce the social relevance

The qualities dealt with in 1 have so far been negative and anti-social. Now comes the challenge to work on the positive elements in personality, which should be more rewarding now that exploration has revealed and, we hope, cleared, the obstacles.

2 This exercise is an entry into imaginative experience via a story, which gives the opportunity for participants to get outside themselves and explore other forms of interaction and reaction in atmospheres outside the naturalistic. If you start by setting the scene you can stimulate creative ideas and also help involvement.

Note the relevance of a), c) and d) to history studies as they are a comparison of then and now (see also d) of *To begin with*).

3 The concentration exercise of handling an imaginary object is a springboard for a variety of situations or stories, each needing the fleshing out of detail from the 5 'W's and, particularly in this case, from relationships where interaction can trigger a variety of attitudes and feelings.

There is scope for inventive ideas in c): for example a legacy, disputed ownership, price, authenticity, how to use, how to dispose of, a prize?

In exercise h), to spur genuineness of the reaction, it would be better if the participant does not know whether the items are stolen or not.

Exercises i) and j) may be combined, with input from movement, music and dance helping to heighten the sensitivity.

4 This exercise involves the challenge of exploring a story, with both stimuli to and demands on the feelings. Without depreciating the unexpected, some preparation would be useful to establish settings, characters, etc. As with 2, it is desirable to build up stimuli so that interest and enthusiasm can be kindled and ideas germinated.

5 The story here will develop its own structure and rationale, but thinking beforehand can be helpful as can some inventive ideas. For example in c) what is the 'it' in his pocket? Is it the missing object or a gun? Looking for additional creativity, one would expect the group to be able to suggest openings of their own, for further stories.

And to follow

1 Perhaps Mr Lonely was originally Mr Selfish. What other reasons could make him lonely? Devise and enact situations which show how he became Mr Lonely from being:

a) Mr Moaner
b) Mr Neglected
c) Mr Ungrateful
d) Mr Bossy
e) Mr Jealous

Devise situations which show the characteristics of these anti-social qualities (as Mr, Miss, etc.): Impatience, Suspicion, Intolerance, Dissatisfaction, Fault-finding, Nosiness, Fractiousness, Daftness, Unforgivingness, Impudence

Now work on their opposites?

2 Try out these ghost situations:

a) a ghost from a former age enters a modern kitchen
b) two climbers meet a ghost
c) a costume tells a story
d) the mirror reflects a former scene
e) once a year a ghost re-appears at:
   • the pier
   • the railway station
   • the scene of the crime
   • the airfield
   • the old farm

3 Imagine you are holding a vase. Visualise it, feel its weight, texture etc. Then use it in the following circumstances:

a) as a valued gift
b) a tutor is talking to a student about it
c) there is a quarrel over...
d) someone is trying to sell it
e) a customer breaks it
f) it sparks off jealousy

g) it is a fake
h) it is stolen goods
i) it is part of a ritual ceremony
j) it is magic

4 There is a knock at the door. Imagine:

a) it is in enemy territory
b) it interrupts the argument
c) the person outside says he is a canvasser
d) that help is needed
e) someone refusing to open the door

5 With each member of the group, in turn, adding a few sentences, a story can be built up, then done, from these beginnings:

a) Angela knew, as soon as she smelt the toast burning, that today was going to be one of those days when everything went wrong
b) Billy had never worked a machine of this sort before
c) he looked round at each of them, but was unable to explain why it was in his pocket
d) George strode forward firmly; but his calm exterior concealed the apprehension inside him
e) as she lifted the receiver she knew it would not be easy

Old Ben

The power of this poem lies in the fact that we are not given any idealised or romantic portrait of this old man. Nor is he a mere 'Mr Lonely'. Instead, he seems to be grafted in to this decaying garden: as much a part of its atmosphere as the mouldering thatch and the mossy trees. From his own decay (and despite it!) seems to exude an almost vibrant sense of frustrated uselessness, perhaps best exemplified in the creepiness of lines 23 and 24:

> His restless thoughts pass to and fro
> but nowhere stay.

The result is a specimen, and a fascinating study for analysis.

Strangely enough (or is it?) I have found quite young children identify easily with this character, or, at any rate, understand his predicament. The insight into his personality leads, from a drama point of view, into the experience of his thoughts, feelings and attitudes as the participant steps into his shoes; and from that root further exploration flowers.

Old Ben

Sad is old Ben Thistlethwaite
Now his day is done,
And all his children
Far away are gone.

He sits beneath his jasmined porch,
His stick between his knees,
His eyes fixed, vacant,
On his moss-grown trees

Grass springs in the green path,
His flowers are lean and dry,
His thatch hangs in wisps against
The evening sky.

He has no heart to care now,
Though the winds will blow,
Whistling in his casement,
And the rain drip through.

He thinks of his old Bettie,
How she would shake her head and say,
'You'll live to wish my sharp old tongue
Could scold – some day.'

But as in pale autumn skies
The swallows float and play,
His restless thoughts pass to and fro,
But nowhere stay.

Soft, on the morrow, they are gone;
His garden then will be
Denser and shadier and greener,
Greener the moss-grown tree.

(Walter de la Mare)

Questions/suggestions

a)   This question introduces the primary consideration of Ben's basic role in the poem.

b) and c)   These questions dig and delve to create a background and to give more fullness to his whole situation. It is interesting to see if, in their inventions, Ben's earlier life and his attitudes at that time show any continuity with his present position. There is a challenge to think back imaginatively into the past, and considerable scope for the participant who will be working on Bettie. Can she make the jump between then and now? Compare her (in her early days) with Beatie in Chapter 1.

d)   This exercise should key in a crucial understanding of the underlying emotions and frustrations inside the man. It can also be a reflection of the feelings and moods *about* what he is thinking. Notice if the nature of thoughts provides triggers for the motivation of Ben's general outlook .

e)   This question deals with the practical action around the character, using other or extra versions of his situation, so giving scope for variation of experience by the participants. Situations suggested here should gain from the insight the poem gives into the way the old man's personality can be interpreted, but perhaps more importantly give further perception into his case. What has made him what he is? All the examples are designed to give opportunity for the use of feelings and attitudes by both partners. Try to spur inventive ideas here and think of other examples; for example the visitor in ii) could be someone who has harboured a grudge over the years (or who knows something incriminating about Ben?); the returning offspring in viii) could have been estranged but is now seeking reconciliation.

If there is a life for Ben beyond the poem, the work done on the suggestions in e) can even produce something of a rehabilitation!

Questions/suggestions

a) In what ways does Ben match his garden?

b) Give the man a background: for example, what was his job when he was younger, when did Bettie die, how old are his children and where are they now?

c) Re-create Bettie, then, and as she might be now. Suppose she were the subject of the poem instead of him? How would the poem describe her?

d) 'His restless thoughts pass to and fro': give some examples of what these thoughts might be. Try an exercise with Old Ben sitting alone and thinking aloud (a soliloquy).

e) Imagine that Ben is joined by another person. They talk together. The other person could be:
   i)   another old man
   ii)   someone he hasn't seen for many years
   iii) someone who tries to cheer him up
   iv)   someone complaining
   v)   a helpful neighbour
   vi)   a younger person, who wants to interview him
   vii) an old lady looking for a friend
   viii) one of his children returning
   ix)   a salesman
   x)   a ghost

6 To begin with

1 This exercise is about the beginning of a relationship. The external stimulus of the other person triggers a reaction which involves an attitude. Exercises a)–e) could have fairly immediate, almost automatic responses.

Exercises f)–j) may need a longer time to work on the motives and the attitudes. These are exercises which investigate the various motives and approaches which can underlie a variety of basic relationships. Other roles, in addition to the child and mother, can be thought of, and further variety and definition can come from feeding in feelings and establishing contexts. For example the mother is angry (because...?), the child is sulky (why?), it is pouring with rain outside, etc.

2 The intention of the interview is to draw out details of the relationship to help to create it and to foster awareness of it. The fact that there are two people being interviewed should help the generation of ideas and this bridging improvisation could easily lead into fuller interaction between the two, based on the facts which emerge during the interview.

Note the scope for variety and inventiveness of situations behind the seemingly generalised suggestions. In g), for example 'opposed each other' could refer to a fight, a sporting occasion, an argument, a competition, rivalry for a girlfriend, a marriage, a strike, an election, etc.

3 This begins with creative concentration from a deliberate task, then widens through oral description to improvisation. The first part can be done as an individual exercise or can be shared out among four people. As with many of these exercises, probing and questioning of what has been imagined will usually bring out more than has originally been given.

The background, b)–d), of these imagined characters provides a basic drama context, so that e) can operate with genuine motivated interaction, and realistic relationships. A further

variable can be provided by variation in the circumstances; for example, it might start to rain, or the bus is late. It would be interesting to see if a 'group feeling ' develops, as does happen in real life. There is scope for imagination in the relationships: for example, among the people you might meet in the queue could be your former teacher, a former wife or husband, an acquaintance you have been forbidden to see, a boyfriend's parents (who don't know you).

4 The development of this exercise will depend on the response of the person being asked. Try a)–e) first, in a literal way; then provide a context. 'Where' is the seat changing taking place (in the cinema, library or bus?) 'When' is the concert? 'Why' do you want someone to get out of the way? 'What' is so interesting about Pat? 'Who' is being asked to give her or himself up? Who are 'you': a girlfriend? the mother? an accomplice? a priest? The initial relationship should be again, almost automatic. It can then be taken further as other facts and circumstances are fed in. With each section, there is the need to find out more about the relationship by working on it.

In exercises f)–g) the difference is that a hurdle has been created: the difficulty of asserting a point of view or making a convincing explanation or excuse. Look therefore for conviction in the person doing the explaining; this should overcome the hurdle, and drive on the relationship.

5 This exercise can be done by one person using two hands or by two people working with each other. It is best done in a relaxed atmosphere. For a change, you could move to the particular from the abstract, that is to full drama situations where the relationships exemplify the contrasts and developments already worked on.

To begin with

1 When sweeping a path, what do you think, feel, say or do when:
  a) the boss rebukes you
  b) the boss praises you
  c) a child mocks you
  d) you see someone you wish to please
  e) you see someone you don't wish to meet

When a mother wants a child to go on an errand:
She can:
  f) order
  g) ask
  h) beg
  i) reason
  j) bribe
And the child can:
  k) agree
  l) refuse
  m) dodge the question
  n) explain why he or she can't
  o) explain what he or she would rather do

Devise situations to show this. Then think of others.

2 Interview two people who have:

  a) gone on holiday together then split up halfway through
  b) swapped jobs
  c) helped each other
  d) been jealous of each other
  e) been involved in a rescue
  f) shared the honours
  g) opposed each other
  h) been sent off together
  i) given good reports about each other
  j) divorced

3 Visualise four people in a bus queue and all that is around them:
  a) describe their appearance, their clothes etc.
  b) what mood do they seem to be in? Why?
  c) give a time of day and give each character a background
  d) tap into their thoughts as they 'think aloud'
  e) four members of the group should become the characters – and converse

4 Ask her or him:

  a) to change seats
  b) to come to the concert
  c) to tell you about Pat
  d) to get out of the way
  e) to give her/himself up

Explain why (to the person concerned, then to others):
  f) you should have more pocket money
  g) you think the proposal is unsuitable
  h) you insulted the Geography teacher on a late night phone-in
  i) you don't want to go out with him or her again
  j) your friend should go to church with you

5 Imagine a conversation between hands which involves:
  a) a request or rejection
  b) an appeal or help
  c) weakness or strength
  d) an idea or a variation or development of it
  e) hope or fulfilment

79

The teacher's problem

I have found situations involving persuasion particularly suitable for bringing into the open attitudes that set up a relationship. Paradoxically, the fact that there is an 'official' student-teacher relationship seems to throw in to greater relief the personal one, by providing a focus in which the interrelating attitudes can operate without distraction.

To think about

This is a consideration of what has happened *after* the initial situation has been worked through. It would be relevant to consider the attitudes the student and teacher originally had towards each other and to compare them to the present ones. It may be that the student never got on with the teacher anyway. Note that the reference to anger, sullenness, etc. applies to both parties.

Variations

Exercises a) and b) suggest further variations to deepen the work on the situation; c) suggests the subtlety of further depth in the motivation; d) brings in a variable from outside and could lead to one of the follow-up exercises.

Follow-up

The follow-up exercise could in turn lead to a variety of other 'school situations', each receiving the same treatment as in *To think about* and *Variations*. Examples could include parent/teacher dispute (whose side is the child on?); teacher/Head teacher conflict about individual pupils; clashes between rugby practice and play rehearsals; the relationships within classes; problems of discipline, homework, bullying, vandalism.

As a final note, it is involvement in the relationship which we want to achieve, not 'who wins the argument'.

The teacher's problem

An art teacher is supervising a class who are drawing pictures of
a vase of flowers. One student, normally a good worker, is sitting
with a blank piece of paper. The teacher has to persuade the pupil
to draw.

To think about

   a) the attitudes the two have to each other
   b) what use, if any, is made of anger, sullenness, coaxing, praise,
      incentives, threats, excuses, reasons
   c) the motives for not drawing
   d) the personal feelings or reactions the teacher may have

Variations

   a) the student is a 'rebellious' one
   b) the teacher is a 'stand in'
   c) one or both of the participants is affected by some recent event
      (e.g. trouble in the family, illness, threat of dismissal, awareness
      of leaving, fear of ridicule)
   d) an inspector is in the room

Follow-up

   a) the headteacher intervenes
   b) the teacher meets the parents
   c) the student conforms but later relapses
   d) other students become involved OR social or medical advice is
      sought
   e) in another situation, the teacher does the same as the student

And to follow

1 The options and variations suggested for the *Trouble with the boss* in Chapter 2 have an obvious relevance here in deepening the details and motivation of the exercise.

2 There are conflicting attitudes but these are also not necessarily on the surface. There could even be a sub text (especially with the completely open situation of e). Therefore you might look for some subtlety in the relationship as it reveals itself (not too quickly). It would be helpful, when working on this, if one partner's attitude was hidden at first; for example, in a) one partner may be concealing his or her taste so as not to hurt the other partner's feelings by immediately voicing an objection.

Exercises f)–j) are different because the varieties of approach are set out beforehand and relationships can be examined in the way they meet the criteria of the initial suggestions. Because there is a basic framework of a relationship, the temptation might be to stereotype and 'impose' the bossiness, etc. To avoid this, analyse the reasons that might lie behind the supportive information that is given. For example, why does the assistant appear inefficient? Is he or she naturally so? Is it the first day in the job? Has the mind been distracted by bad news or good news?

As with any subordinate role (see Chapter 2) the question of how far to be acquiescent and how far to be assertive might arise. How this is resolved, if at all, will depend on the participant's own personality.

3 In this exercise we try to experience relationships through spontaneity, with an examination, if required, in retrospect. It is best done by participants who are by now well used to improvisation work. Note that the initial remark can be spoken by either of the participants and, although the situation begins with two people, you can feed in other characters, spontaneously, as the situation develops. This will elaborate relationships further.

4 The word 'build' does not of course exclude the spontaneous and extra elements which come in to all situations as they develop and personalities interact. As with so many of the exercises, motivation is important and here the situation itself should be the cause of the motive and ensuing attitudes which, taking note of 2 a)–e), need not be immediately apparent on the surface. In fact, as long as they are genuinely experienced by the participant, they need not be 'apparent' at all!

A point to notice in this exercise, and many others involving personal interaction, is whether the body language of the participants matches the intention of the action.

5 This is a more advanced exercise. Not everyone may be able to tackle this, but for those old or mature enough, it is an opportunity to look into motives behind some of the subtleties of more intimate interpersonal relationships, where the inner attitude or sub text may be more important than what is actually said. The field is open for other characters and other variations in the relationships to be suggested, or to develop.

When Jane and Harry later join the group it would be desirable if they have not actually heard what has been said. How many of the original group maintain, on the surface, the same attitudes?

And to follow

1 You are an employer, and an employee:
 a) is asking for a rise or a promotion
 b) left the place untidy OR left work undone
 c) is in dispute over overtime OR involved in a disagreement on policy
 d) is suspected of being 'on the fiddle'
 e) is off work, but is spotted in the high street

2 This action takes place outside a shop:
 a) a brother and sister wish to buy a joint present but their tastes differ
 b) two people are thinking of buying clothes; one is jealous of the other
 c) you are two friends; one of you is short of money
 d) a husband and wife are discussing a present for her mother; they differ
 e) are you thinking what I'm thinking?

Now try these situations inside a shop:
 f) the customer can't make up his or her mind; the assistant is:
 • normal
 • impatient
 • keen to please
 g) the assistant is inefficient but arrogant; the customer is:
 • normal
 • browbeaten
 • not prepared to put up with this
 h) the assistant is inefficient; the customer is:
 • normal
 • bossy
 • understanding
 i) the customer is in a hurry but has a complicated order; the assistant is:
 • very talkative
 • trying to listen to the radio
 • from another country

 j) the customer is really the boss; the assistant is any of the above

3 Someone is packing. Another person enters the room. Using any of the remarks below, continue the situation and see what relationship develops:
 a) 'Get out!'
 b) 'Does Mum know about this?'
 c) 'What do you think you're doing?'
 d) 'I've just heard a police car'
 e) 'It's no good trying to talk me out of it'

4 Build situations which might cause a person to be:
 a) envious of a friend
 b) in a huff at a party
 c) suspicious of his or her intentions
 d) no longer afraid of him
 e) sorry

5 A group of people are discussing the engagement of Jane and Harry. The group includes:
 a) Christine, who used to be engaged to Harry
 b) Isobel, who wishes she was engaged to Harry
 c) Tom, who has had conflicts with Harry
 d) Liz, who knows little of Harry but has a high opinion of Jane
 e) Peter, who wishes he was engaged to Jane
 f) Jane and Harry, who join the group later

What is a wife?

The emphasis is largely on Portia as she challenges her husband's evasions and conduct, making her attitude very obvious as she spells out, by negatives, her view of a wife's relationship. This becomes a challenge to Brutus and an accusation, not only of his behaviour but of his whole concept of her wifely role.

And Brutus? Why does he not wish to tell Portia of his involvement in the assassination plot? He doesn't say much as he blocks and temporises, but what is his sub text? What is running through his mind as she talks, and how does it influence his attitude and feelings towards her? Elucidation of this is the test of the participant's involvement.

'...with an angry wafture', etc. (Line 22) – the general picture of Brutus' behaviour in this section is not complimentary to Portia and does not give a good image of Brutus. The person playing Portia might have a view about this. And what does Brutus think of his behaviour as so described?

'humours' (Line 32) – will probably need explaining

'sick offence', etc. (Line 40) – would Brutus agree with this?

'I charm you' (Line 44) – has more the modern meaning of a'demand'; but in the sense of her fixing a sort of spell on him by her insistence, it might give some indication of the power she feels she has inside herself (see Question a) overleaf).

Previous persuasion exercises are relevant and an obvious comparison is with the following scene (Act 2, Scene 2) between Caesar and Calpurnia. It might be of value, however, both to drama and to other areas of the curriculum, to study further scenes from plays involving relationships within marriage.

What is a wife?

Brutus has become involved in a plot to kill Caesar. His wife, Portia, not knowing this, questions her husband's behaviour. Enter Portia

Portia Brutus, my Lord!

Brutus Portia: what mean you? Wherefore rise you now?
It is not for your health thus to commit
Your weak condition to the raw cold morning.

Portia Nor for yours neither. You have ungently, Brutus,
Stole from my bed: and yesternight at supper
You suddenly arose, and walked about,
Musing and sighing, with your arms across:
And when I asked you what the matter was,
You stared upon me, with ungentle looks.
I urged you further, then you scratched your head,
And too impatiently stamped with your foot:
Yet I insisted, yet you answered not,
But with an angry wafture of your hand
Gave sign for me to leave you: So I did . . .

Brutus I am not well in health, and that is all.

Portia Brutus is wise, and were he not in health,
He would embrace the means to come by it.

Brutus Why so I do; good Portia go to bed.

Portia Is Brutus sick? And is it physical
To walk unbraced, and suck up the humours
Of the dank morning? What, is Brutus sick?
And will he steal out of his wholesome bed
To dare the vile contagion of the Night?

And tempt the rheumy and unpurged air
To add unto his sickness? No, my Brutus,
You have some sick offence within your mind,
Which by the right and virtue of my place
I ought to know of: and upon my knees,
I charm you, by my once commended beauty,
By all your views of Love, and that great vow
Which did incorporate and make us one,
That you unfold to me, yourself, your half,
Why you are heavy . . .

Brutus Kneel not, gentle Portia.

Portia I should not need if you were gentle Brutus.
Within the bond of Marriage, tell me Brutus,
Is it excepted, I should know no secrets
That appertain to you? Am I yourself,
But as it were in sort, or limitation?
To keep with you at meals, comfort your bed,
And talk to you sometimes? Dwell I but in the suburbs
Of your good pleasure? If it be no more,
Portia is Brutus' harlot, not his wife.

(William Shakespeare: *Julius Caesar*,
Act 2 Scene 1)

Questions/suggestions

a) Questions i) and iii) are fairly clearly stated in the text; question ii) is implicit and will have to be deduced by reading between the lines. It is essential, however, for the truth of her involvement, that the person playing Portia is clear about the answer.

b) Again, this is to be deduced. In Portia's train of thought she will have a target: the statement or accusation which she thinks will clinch things. It is this that the rest of the speech builds to. The use of a thought sequence, expressed in own words, is valuable preparation here.

c) The fact that there is a 'why' and a 'how' suggests limitations in Brutus' personality as a whole, but it is the 'why' which will be taxing him inside as he listens through her speeches. Portia, by contrast, is positive, picking up every reply of Brutus to make capital with it (compare with Joan's approach in Chapter 2). Consideration of this should help the answer to a) ii) above.

d) The answer will be the result of Brutus' thoughts and reactions during the scene, and the participant's reply should come before seeing the real reply which follows in the text. But which reply is truer to the Brutus Shakespeare gives us? This is an example of how experience through improvisation can enrich the interpretation of the text as well as vice versa.

e) This is about conspiracy to kill for political reasons; the nearest approach today might be that of the 'terrorist', and it might be worth asking whether his motives are as high minded as were Brutus'; or would we now see Brutus as we see the terrorist? In either case, each has a wife and a relationship. (See also 4 e) of *To begin with*.)

Questions/suggestions

a) What does Portia think and feel about:
- i)   Brutus
- ii) herself
- iii) the role of a wife

b) In what ways does she try to put pressure on Brutus? Which of her remarks might affect Brutus most?

c) How and why does Brutus try to put her off, and how does Portia respond to this?

d) At the end of the speeches, what might Brutus' attitude be to Portia? How might he reply to her final statement?

e) Devise a contemporary version of this situation.

7 To begin with

1 These are concentration exercises to alert the senses, to help the participant become receptive to giving and receiving communication. Structuring through the discipline of shape and pattern should heighten this state. The repeating and copying also reinforces and tests awareness. So, with a)–e), see if a partner, following the eye movements, can reproduce the line of action.

Exercise f) can also be practised with a radio, for example for listening to and repeating the details of a weather forecast.

In exercise g), for training in listening sensitivity, try further refinements, for example picking out different types of vehicle while listening to the traffic outside, or listen to and then describe types of weather.

A possible example for exercise i) could be a group of soldiers approaching: first with uncertainty, caution and stealth, and then pouncing in a rush. This can be conveyed by the sound of footsteps to a group listening with their eyes closed, then translated into other sounds (e.g. drums) and voices (e.g. cries and orders).

2 In this section look for clarity, detail and imagination; but, in a)–e), check how honest the reality of the recollection is; for example, if a car is involved in d) the witness may not remember the number plate, so say this rather than make one up on the spur of the moment. If responses seem too glib, do a spell on literal memory work.

Try differing contexts for eye witness accounts (e.g. to the police, to a teacher, to the family, to a friend) and a variation is to treat the exercise as a commentary.

It might be beneficial to set exercises f)–g) in a more formal context, for example in the form of a lecture to a group, particularly if detail or elaboration is missing. This should ensure that enough preparation will be put in. The use of TV, if you have access to one, would be another stimulating context (see also Chapter 8 *To begin with* Exercise 4). The participants should be prepared to answer questions on their topic.

3 and **4** Shape and patterning come in to these sections, together with orientation, to give a sense of structure. It is often useful as a base for someone who finds communication difficult.

To vary the exercise the directions in 3 a) could be given to someone whose grasp of the language is lacking or by someone who has lost his voice or can only speak another language (try it in French?).

In exercise 3 d) a useful question would be to ask what is being filmed. Note that the positioning of the cameras would need to be directly related to the whole pattern of the event.

5 In this section communication is moving away from the basically literal and physical, to bring in attitudes and feelings and the start of drama contexts. In a)–e) the task has two objectives: to frame the request, and how to persevere if or when it is refused. Basically, how can you manipulate the person? A consideration of the sub text (what is intended but not spoken) may be relevant here. For variation, and as a supporting exercise, a)–e) can also be done on the telephone. Note that there is scope for refusing.

The extent to which the situations in f)–j) move into fuller drama contexts will be determined by the reactions and interaction of whoever receives the advice. Further development could come by extra characters and extra inventive detail to fill out the situation and deepen the relationships. For example to i) could be added: conflicting parents, prospective employer (unsatisfactory?), a friend (tie in with j)?), or a social worker (why?).

To begin with

1 With your eyes, follow the imagined course of:
a) chimney smoke drifting in the air
b) the flight of a butterfly, in slow motion
c) a person entering, fixing a light bulb, then leaving
d) a corner kick
e) someone receiving a prize

Try the following things with your voice and ears:
f) follow an explanation, description or instructions given by another person. Repeat them
g) with your eyes closed, make a list in your mind of all the sounds you can hear in the room. Can you copy them?
h) one group makes a pattern of sounds which has a recognisable form. A second group reproduce this
i) footsteps can tell a story. Try to make a story in groups, listening then reproducing. Then try with other sounds, and voices
j) pass on a message: close to, then further away, then further still. Put it in a situation, for example calling from the shore

2 Give eye-witness accounts of:
a) a dog running loose in a store
b) a bull loose in a market place
c) a fire
d) a raid
e) a rescue

Explain and demonstrate:
f) how to get from your house to...
g) a recipe, or how to use a...
h) a pattern, in sewing or woodwork
i) a skill in sport
j) how to set out: a workshop, a craft room, a studio, a laboratory

3 Draw a map or plan of your school or local area and use it as a basis to:
a) give directions to a visitor to get from one point to another
b) explain the route of a procession to those leading it
c) instruct a squad of soldiers where to take up their positions
d) direct a TV camera crew on the best positions for filming
e) outline to a group of motorists a new traffic scheme

4 Devise routine actions (and words where appropriate) that could happen:
a) at a hospital bed
b) by a café table
c) on a milk round
d) around an office desk
e) in an allotment

5 Devise situations for asking favours:

a) of a friend: to lend you some cash
b) of your mother: to bring home a friend of whom she disapproves
c) of your father: to use his machine
d) of your brother or sister: to borrow a pen, bracelet or radio
e) of a group: to turn the volume down

Give advice in the following situations:
f) on which cooker to choose
g) on setting out a garden
h) on the wisdom of not being a borrower
i) on staying at school, or leaving
j) on the suitability, or otherwise, of a companion

89

Captured and taken

This situation has been chosen because of its inclusiveness; it is a large and convenient framework for various activities, relationships and incidents that involve free and functional communication.

To think about

The key to successful believability is the motivation and attitude of those taking part. For instance what is the basic relationship between the prisoner and the kidnappers: is he or she obedient or truculent or what towards them? What is *their* approach? Note the differing personalities and other pairs of relationships: for example the kidnappers to each other; the hostage to the girl or boyfriend or to the wife or to the parents and the family; the parent to the other parent (e.g. is there disagreement over how to approach the crisis?). Note other inventive details; for example, maybe the parents are divorced so could one parent, in fact, be involved in the abduction? Is the hostage famous? Is the hostage a member of the royal family?

Speech activities

There is a close relationship here with the *To begin with* exercises, and the exercises in interviewing done in previous chapters. There could be a consideration of social pressures (press, TV, neighbours, etc.) or even an international dimension. When the police question the kidnappers we should learn more about the reasons for the crime.

The action

All the activities so far should provide material for the important missing part of the story, that is what actually happened. Hints are given in the exercises for the development of the story, but there is scope for further inventiveness, either planned or spontaneous; for example: mistaken identity.

Finally, though the situation has the outline and characteristics of an adventure story, we are really examining, through the experiencing of it, how the thoughts, attitudes, feelings and actions of the participants within the story relate to each other by communication. Perception of how they do it is the test, and the use of it is the fruition.

Captured – and taken

At the start of the situation, a young person is kidnapped or taken hostage and the police (or military) are called in. At the end, there is an escape or a rescue. But what happens in the middle?

To think about

a) Why is the kidnapping taking place, and where?
b) What are the backgrounds and varying personalities of those concerned
c) Is there any scope for communication between those involved, especially the prisoner and the captors. What are their thoughts, feelings and relationships as well as words?
d) How will the action proceed? Consider ideas for a story outline.

Speech activities

To build detail into the infrastructure, you could try the speech activities:
a) eye witness accounts, and interviews with family and friends
b) telephone contact, during the captivity and after the escape
c) when safe, how the story is told to:
   • the family
   • the friend/s
   • the police
   • the press
   • a television reporter
d) the police interrogate the captured kidnappers

The action

Points to bear in mind are:
a) the type of preparation made by kidnappers, a discussion of their motives and methods, plotting of the victim's movements
b) the activities and situations during the story. This involves actions, locations (here or abroad?) and other people. Was use made of telephone calls, letters or ransom strategies? Have there been any earlier, unsuccessful, attempts at escape?
c) what steps were taken by the police? What are their suspicions? Have they any clues? Do they use the local radio and TV? Are mistakes made by the kidnappers?
d) how does the hostage get away? Does he or she use their own initiative, or are they helped by friends or the police? Are there any accidents? Are the kidnappers captured? How? Does this happen straightaway or after further action?

And to follow

1 This section comprises the spade work for enacted situations. It resembles the previous one and looks at detail, character, relationships and incidents for an inclusive context. The use of locations should be a support. Communication in the interviews may be largely functional at first, then the characters can be freer in the enactment. Although there can be considerable building of material to begin with, it is important that the progress of each situation is then given its head to find its own level.

2 More structure is given in this section, but the background of characters, etc. is just as important. The danger is to preconceive what is going to happen, so it has been deliberately left open ended. Note that a 'knock at the door' can be the start of many drama situations: the context of the door leads to the situation's development.

3 This section gives practice in the 'organisation' of communication through group discussion, committee work, marshalling of arguments, etc., and gives the shy person a chance to take part but to 'hide' until he or she is ready to say more. The participants may have personal experience of committee work in school activities, but some guidance may be required.

Knowledge of committee procedures is a valuable social skill, but the more formal contexts should not preclude personal attitudes and relationships arising from commitment and strength of feeling. These may include views on social welfare for example or other views expressed in freer public and political discussions, such as are seen on television.

Participants will probably suggest other social issues, maybe relevant to their own area. This can be a spin off to social studies. A trip to a local council meeting would be relevant?

4 The exercises in this section are to devise situations which impose demands on the 'you'. But who is the 'you'? The answer to this will affect each situation because of personality interaction. There is scope for varied contexts, and varying outcomes could arise from each because of the different attitudes and standpoints that could come from the 'you' (and the 'him, 'her' and 'them').

These questions might help to develop the situations in c), d), e), h):

  c) Are Mrs Stokes' rumours true – and how do they affect you?
  d) How do you normally get on with Hargreaves?
  e) The obvious question about Caroline is 'why?'. And who is Katie?
  h) The biggest demand will be informing the 'other' parent.

5 The objective in this section is to build personal communication situations. Creative details are needed to flesh out the bare framework of each exercise with locations, personality, action, motivation, feelings, attitudes and relationships. Attitudes need not necessarily be on the surface, they may be present instead in a sub text.

Exercises f)–j) can be either spontaneous or planned, but the remarks should be sufficient to begin to create situations involving clash or compromise, where a decision has to be reached. There is scope for putting in variables (other people, other circumstances) to add variety and deepen the progress towards a conclusion. There is also scope for the group to invent further 'remarks' to set up more communication situations.

And to follow

1 Investigate the personalities and interview all the people concerned as a build up to an enactment of:
a) a conflict at the customs
b) a theft at the party
c) a spy in the office
d) a rescue on the bridge
e) accusations in the car park

2 A young person is left in charge of a garage while the owner is at lunch:
a) there are incoming telephone calls
b) several customers visit
c) the police phone to warn of a dangerous character calling at garages
d) there is a phone call from the young person to the owner
e) there is a knock at the door

3 You are in the following situations:

a) the city chief outlines, to a public meeting, the plans for a new development. There are critics
b) there is a meeting to discuss the borough's education system. Inner city representatives query the provision for education, recreation and social welfare
c) the transport committee discusses how to improve the traffic arrangements
d) the town has been bequeathed a large sum of money and a public enquiry is held to discuss how to spend it
e) a 'hung' council (equally balanced between two political parties) is debating a controversial issue. At the end of the debate the impartial chairman has the casting vote

4 Now try these situations:

a) Doris wants to help you. You would prefer Shirley
b) Harry wants to do the job which you regard as yours
c) is it true that Mrs Stokes has been spreading these rumours?
d) Mr Hargreaves is putting up an extension. You object
e) you know that Caroline is not a good companion for Katie. How can you tell Katie? (or warn off Caroline?)
f) you'd like to repair the rift with Susan
g) George isn't the person he used to be.
h) which parent should you go on holiday with?
i) Jean (or Joe) wants help. But you said last time: never again
j) tell the Thorntons:
• you're sorry to disappoint them
• they have a cheek
• it had better not happen again
• what their boy was doing
• you need their help

5 And for contrasts:

a) one is keen to go, the other reluctant
b) one wishes for information, the other is fed up with questioning
c) one is an optimist, the other is a pessimist
d) one fancies himself or herself, the other doesn't fancy him or her
e) one wishes to concentrate, the other to communicate

And in the following remarks:
f) he'll never agree to it
g) I'm afraid
h) it is a waste of money!
i) she wants to see you
j) but you'll have to take part

Girls' talk

Associated with communication is the lack of it. Even if explicit words or explanations are wanting, contact still has to be made if there is the need.

In this extract, the 2nd girl is communicating unconsciously. She doesn't understand rationally the depths of what she is saying to her companion, so her excitement and fears are revealed in hints and allusiveness and symbols, which mean nothing to the 1st girl, who only reacts to the literal level of the remarks.

Note that although the character of the 2nd girl may not be aware of the implications of what she is saying, the participant should be, but should not show this. It is her sub text (see a) overleaf), kept subsumed by her simple but serious enthusiasm which drives the character along.

The drama exemplification comes in the contrast of the characters and in their relationship. This can be brought out by the improvisation of smaller situations involving clashes of attitude (e.g. enthusiasm for something versus the wet blanket approach; recounting a story to someone who picks holes in it; a dreamer talking to a disbeliever). In such instances the onus is on one person to get through to the other though that person may not be sure how to express it fully. Note the relevance of exercises 5 f)–j) of *And to follow* and any exercise involving sub texts and coded language.

A sociological and literary study of examples of pop culture (e.g. teenage magazines) is a relevant spin off to the work on this play.

Girls' talk

Two teenage girls are chatting outside a sweet shop.

2nd Girl Walking through seaweed – it's like on a tight-rope – all slippery – and you got to walk carefully . . . Some of it looks like them straps of liquorice. And some, when you walk on it, goes off pop! . . .

1st Girl I seen that sort. You can make it pop.

2nd Girl Yep. You can pop it if you stand on it hard enough.

1st Girl I popped it myself sometimes. You know, with my shoes on.

2nd Girl Well, some of the seaweed – it's that funny pop-stuff, and others is kind of longer . . . You got to walk on it very carefully or maybe you'd slip . . . So you hold your arms out.

1st Girl How?

2nd Girl Well, like the lady did on the tight-rope. Holding your arms out – that helps you balance – but you got to take just small steps . . . or you'd maybe fall.

1st Girl I never went in for walking through seaweed. Well, I have walked through. But just with my shoes on.

2nd Girl That aint *really* walking through seaweed.

1st Girl I'll tell you something, it can spoil your shoes.

2nd Girl I always take my shoes off.

1st Girl So far as I'm concerned, you can keep that seaweed.

2nd Girl Maybe you have to walk through seaweed – if you want to get past the seaweed and down to the sea.

1st Girl There's a lot of it grows on top of the rocks.

2nd Girl There's a lot of it grows all over the seaside. And if you want to get where the sea is, well you've got to walk through it . . . But you've got to walk careful . . .

1st Girl Yep. It can ruin a pair of shoes.

2nd Girl Not if you take them off and carry them.

1st Girl That's OK for you – you aint *scared* of seaweed.

2nd Girl What's to be scared of in seaweed?

1st Girl I dunno. You can't see though . . .

2nd Girl Yep. You can't see what's in seaweed. I like that. It's sort of exciting . . .

1st Girl You got funny ideas of what's exciting . . .

(Ian Hamilton Finlay: *Walking through Seaweed*)

Questions/suggestions

a)   The answer lies in the interpretation of the word 'seaweed'.

b)   The participant probably will understand. Her task is to make the character's incomprehension believable to herself. To aid this, try the exercises suggested on the previous page; a 'wilful' determination not to be persuaded or deluded can be helpful.

c)   An attachment to material things and considerations, plus the literal interpretation of any question or demand, can be a useful block in the task referred to in b).

d)   The surface answer is obvious enough. But if one probes this relationship further, as the 2nd girl continues to press her point, there is considerable potential for development of 1st girl, both from a dramatic and a personal viewpoint.

e)   In this question there is an opportunity to match the sensitivity of movement and tactile communication to the play's theme in order to highlight the communication relationship. This is an example of a flexibility which can also be used with the setting and the general action.

Questions/suggestions

a) What is the 2nd girl trying to tell the 1st girl? Why doesn't she tell her directly? Find one remark that might sum up what she is really wanting to communicate.

b) Does the 1st girl understand?

c) 'It can ruin a pair of shoes': how does this sum up what is in the 1st girl's mind?

d) What might the 1st girl think of the 2nd girl? Why?

e) Take the part of the 2nd girl and lead the 1st girl through seaweed on the seashore, as described in the dialogue. Show the 1st girl what you mean when you say things like '... You got to walk on it very carefully or maybe you'd slip ... So you hold your arms out'.

8 To begin with

1 This section puts participants in at the deep end, standing up for themselves both on defence and attack, but from a base of careful and reasoned thought. Each participant has to be clear on his or her point of view and able to support it in depth. Hence preparation is needed for each of the exercises which can be demanding because of the nature of the 'opponent'. Preparation will include organising the facts, making notes and remembering.

2 This section is based on orientation and memory, and encourages a feel for the detail in pattern and structure with, again, the need for the participant to sort out a coherent stand for himself or herself in a social interrelationship.

3 In this section invention is needed to give the background (what happened) behind each occurrence. This time the self justification, backed we would hope by rational argument, can move into a fuller drama situation with a social reference, where perhaps more than one point of view will emerge which can be appreciated by the participants.

4 In this section the variety of focuses for the demonstration or explanation should help confidence, give experience of adaptability and produce a similar variety in the deliveries, thus widening the participant's ability to cope. Some of the situations might impose considerable demands on the participant's resources, therefore it is important that this exercise is not rushed. If participants are finding it difficult it is advisable to stop the action and work on the details of the topic (e.g. know exactly what items are in the recipe, what to do with them, where, and plan each step and how it will be delivered).

5 The emphasis in this section is on a rational objection or query rather than on an angry confrontation. Therefore we must assume that the applicant is keen to have the job, because then he or she will be sincere, and has the challenge of expressing his or her views and disagreements in a non-provocative way. Participants will also gain more experience in the social skills of the job interview (see also *Holding an interview*, Chapter 1).

To begin with

1 You are having an argument with:

a) someone you have never met before
b) your girlfriend when she expects you to stand up for her
c) some people who are demanding that you join in
d) someone who is challenging the leader
e) someone you think is victimising you
f) the careers teacher
g) the social worker OR probation officer
h) the doctor or psychiatrist
i) the boss
j) someone who is not pulling his or her weight

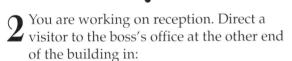

2 You are working on reception. Direct a visitor to the boss's office at the other end of the building in:

a) a hospital
b) a hotel
c) an office block
d) a school or college
e) an airport

Then, as the visitor, when you reach the other end, explain why you have come.

3 Explain why you:

a) took the blame
b) let the others lead you
c) broke the curfew
d) allowed him to get away with it
e) could stand it no longer

Now re-enact each situation with the other characters involved.

4 Using imaginary ingredients, demonstrate and explain how you would prepare a special meal from a recipe to:
a) the rest of the group
b) a TV camera (or object representing this) OR a radio listener
c) an examiner (or similar expert)
d) someone who has difficulty understanding
e) your closest friend

Then explain and demonstrate, with similar options, the following:
f) how you would cut the crime rate
g) a model you have made OR how something works
h) new clothes
i) your attack on (or defence of) the Church
j) exercises or methods in physical fitness or dance, or a sport

Be prepared to answer questions or face arguments about your demonstrations.

5 You are being interviewed for a job and:

a) you insist on certain conditions
b) you have criticisms of the training scheme that goes with the job
c) you object when they ask you about:
 • your way of life
 • your religion
 • your politics
 • your family
 • your schooling
d) you feel you need to know more about the job OR you feel they are concealing something
e) you feel that unfair bias is being shown from one of the members of the interviewing panel

99

In the hot seat

This is a group interview based on a true happening. Questions by the group can be prepared at first, but the replies they receive should generate further questioning, and, maybe, accusations.

To think about

The personality of the teenager is at the core of this section. Is his or her attitude one of bravado, belonging to a 'hard case', or one of someone normally conformist?

    a) Detail on this forms the base for the rest of the exercise.

    b) Is this a salutory experience, or an education in crime? Some research could be done on prison life, or the imagination could be aided by the experience of time spent in confinement.

    c) This is the crux of the situation, with opportunity to investigate aspects of personality within a social framework.

    d) What will be the outcome of a)–c)? Will the teenager 'grow'?

Do the parents present a joint front or do they differ in their views and in their relationship to the teenager? It could be interesting to see whether they accept any responsibility or blame for what has happened, and how far righteous (or self righteous) justification operates. Both approaches can be 'correct', depending on their respective backgrounds, life-styles, relationships, etc. Resolutions for the future in b) could reinforce and clarify the parents' attitude, either from a caring or a repressive point of view. Feelings about the neighbours in c) could be determined by their backgrounds or references to social class.

Note that the outlook and attitudes of the parents here is often influenced (even created) by the spontaneous reaction to the questions and the approach of the questioners. The parents in this situation are often seen by a young audience as 'the guilty ones'.

Follow-up

What has gone before should provide background material and an insight into the personalities of the participants so family and social situations can be enacted.

Finally, should the parents and the teenager collude in establishing a background beforehand? To some extent it is a good idea, particularly on facts (e.g. the parents' occupation and the type of neighbourhood where they live). It would be useful for the teenager to know the parents' background, but in real life the reverse doesn't always apply; parents may know less about their offspring's activities. Therefore the attitudes and feelings from the parents are more likely to be genuine if some aspects of the episode are unexpected.

In the hot seat

A teenager who has been in prison on remand for smoking cannabis (and is now on probation) is being questioned by the group. So are the parents.

To think about

You are the teenager:

a) What is your background (home, school, friends) and was this case a one-off or a regular occurrence?
b) What did you think of prison life and what, if anything, did you learn from it?
c) Be clear on your attitude to your parents, teachers and friends. Is it any different now from before the drugs episode?
d) How do you see your future?

You are the parents:

a) Fill in the details of your background also. For example how do you see yourselves as parents? Do you accept any blame for what has happened? How did you bring up your family? Were you soft, or too hard? Are there any brothers or sisters in your family? How were you brought up?
b) What is your present attitude to your child? Will you make any changes to the way you treat her or him, and how you will bring up the rest of the family now?
c) What is the attitude of friends and neighbours? Have there been any changes?
d) What has been for you the worst aspect of this case?

Follow-up
a) Re-enact the original situation, the trial, and the interviews with social workers, etc.
b) Try out some family relationship situations.
c) What is the future of the teenager? Will there be any difficulties; for example, problems with employment, or relationships, etc?
d) What is the effect on brothers, sisters or friends?

101

And to follow

1 As has been seen often before when building up a situation we would be looking for a mixture of the prepared and the spontaneous; the latter often giving the kick start the situation might require.

2 This section should give some food for the imagination as it involves the dramatisation of social situations or stories from a particular stimulus. It is important to build up the stimulus beforehand (and play the music if possible) so that interest and enthusiasm can be kindled and ideas germinated. In addition to suggesting a theme, music is also helpful to indicate mood, atmosphere and setting. There is scope for other song titles suggested by members of the group.

3 These are basically problems between people. In working through them, the individual's awareness of his own attitude and feelings is more important than any apparent 'solutions'. Note that this applies to all the people in the situation and not just the 'you'. As an example, examine the motives of the person doing the 'victimising'. How would he justify this? Would he regard it *as* 'victimising'? Working with each individual in this way will help to develop sensitivity to the relationships and the issues involved.

Possibly e) is the most problematical of the situations contained in 3 because it requires the most sensitivity. The biggest danger is to caricature and over simplify the situation. To prevent this, work on the detail of the previous background of the characters, take special note of the caveats in the previous paragraph, and use the element of surprise, (for example make the person playing Jimmy unaware of Andrew and the cinema). This could be an approximation to the uncertainty and ambivalence of this situation in real life.

4 There is a close connection with the arguments in *To begin with*. The key is in the conflict, and, if properly involved, each member should feel the *need* to communicate a point of view, which will make that need recognisable and give the action believability. Members of the group will probably be able to suggest other family relationships and further variations within these situations, especially when looking for details of motive. For example in c), why do the parents disapprove? There could be many reasons given, but suppose the parents had found out that (unknown to their daughter or son) the boy or girlfriend had previously been in trouble with the police?

5 Devise clear contexts (5 'W's) for these social situations and keep the framework tight by close attention to detail; within this, motivation can drive the action.

b) There are varied options for Jenny: for example she herself does not have this trouble; she disagrees with Linda's interpretation (she may fancy Linda's boyfriends); shall she tell Linda the truth (about Linda herself; about the boyfriends)? Shall she give genuine advice?

d) Abortion and arranged marriages are obvious topics (in addition to basic differences in beliefs and procedures; for example should it be a church wedding or not? There are also situations elsewhere.

e) It would be useful if one partner does not really know that the other is pretending.

And to follow

1 Try these situations prompted by the following remarks:
a) 'I'm not prepared to help you'
b) 'But I trusted you'
c) 'I daren't tell them'
d) 'You're too young'
e) 'Did she not tell you?'

2 Make up stories, situations or relationships from the following song titles:
a) The girl of my best friend
b) We'll meet again
c) She's leaving home
d) The day I met Marie
e) It's a sin

3 What might happen when:

a) a friend of yours is victimising another friend of yours. All three of you meet
b) the daughter says she is going to a friend's party, but her mother had expected her to visit relations
c) a new member of the team is upsetting everyone, yet you need that member
d) someone you were rude to yesterday at lunch you later find has helped you; today you are at lunch together
e) Jimmy's girlfriend, Susan, went to the cinema with Andrew when Jimmy was away. When he returns:
  • on Monday, Jimmy meets her in town
  • on Tuesday, Andrew asks her to come to a concert on Saturday afternoon
  • on Wednesday, Jimmy receives tickets for the same concert and decides to ask Susan
  • on Thursday, Susan is asked by Laura to participate in a sports fixture on the Saturday afternoon
  • on Friday, Susan wants to go to the disco. Only one of her friends (above) is free

So what happens on the Saturday?

4 Try out these situations in the family:

a) the son wishes to leave school and join the army. His parents are both ardent pacifists. Will he join up?
b) two sisters are after the same boyfriend. But who is he after?
c) the parents disapprove of their daughter's boyfriend (or son's girlfriend). But what does the boy or girlfriend think?
d) the husband objects to his wife going to evening classes. Will she go?
e) the daughter is against her mother's new husband-to-be. What is his reaction?

5 You are in the following situations:

a) police question you about your friend and a crime. You know he is guilty. They don't
b) Linda is telling Jenny about the poor quality of her boyfriends, and looks for her advice, support and sympathy. Is Jenny happy to give this?
c) you meet a half brother or sister you hadn't met or heard of before, although he or she has heard of you
d) a boy and girl find religion coming between them
e) your flat mate is in a bad mood, but is pretending not to be

103

Holiday meeting

What is unsaid, thought about and listened to, is probably more revealing than the actual dialogue. Each character has problems (loneliness, shyness, defensiveness, lack of confidence, low self esteem, etc.) which they are not open about but which can be diagnosed through an improvisational working on the text. The sub text is therefore important.

Enid, behind her front of street-wise insouciance, has the task of listening closely to diagnose Norman's situation. Norman, by contrast, has to avoid being too perceptive of Enid, as this will interfere with the barrier of self-deprecation he has erected.

'What you come here for?'(Line 17) – this is the third time she has asked this. What progression and variation has there been in her mind, which will influence her expression?

(*Quickly*) (Line 25) – this is an indication of Enid's cover up, and a rare example of a stage direction which gives creative insight into the play.

(*Very casual*) (Line 29) – this is similarly illustrative. In her sub text, Enid is more interested than she wants to admit. Ask the participant why?

Holiday meeting

Norman and Enid meet each other while on holiday at the seaside. Norman is an office worker; Enid is a factory worker. They are on the pier, outside a dance hall.

Norman I can tell you weeks in advance what sort of time I'll have. *(Pause. Semi soliloquy)* . . . I know it. I know it . . . I know it'll be terrible. By about Tuesday I'll have been everywhere, seen the shows, looked at the beach, had my photograph taken . . . All the things I did last year. *(Pause)* Makes it easier, you see, I can put anything I like on the postcards . . . nothing's going to happen. I'll be glad when it's over.

Enid *(Baffled)* What you come for?

Norman It's my holiday.

Enid What you come for, if it's lousy?

Norman You need the change, you know, a break from the routine. Routine in the office, it drives you mad. Nine o'clock you get there, read the paper, have tea, answer the mail, talk about last night's telly, go for dinner, read the early edition, have tea, answer the afternoon mail, talk about the next lot of telly, go home . . . *(Pause)* Watch telly. It's terrible.

Enid *(Sympathetic for the first time)* What you come here for?

Norman This . . . this is terrible in a different sort of way. You need the change . . . Break in routine. I suppose it sounds silly . . .

Enid *(Puzzled)* You what?

Norman Silly . . . I suppose it sounds silly.

Enid No. It isn't silly. *(Pause)* The reason it's lousy . . . it's because you're by yourself.

Norman Yes . . .

Enid *(Quickly)* Course I'm with Jean, my friend, you'd like Jean.

Norman I used to have a friend. I used to have three . . .

Enid I always go dancing with Jean. It's a good way to meet people.

Norman *(Slight bitterness)* Three friends.

Enid *(Very casual)* What happened? They get married?

Norman How do you know?

Enid Blokes of your age, they're usually married.

Norman *(Taken aback)* What do you mean? My age?

(Alan Plater: *See the Pretty Lights*)

Questions/suggestions

a) Enid's questions cause Norman to reveal a great deal. Yet she is not a professional psychiatrist. Her results seem to be gained from straightforward natural curiosity about the man and how he deviates from her (limited) 'norm'; she *is* genuinely puzzled. She is unconsciously incisive from a defensive base.

b) This is an example of improvisation around the characters. The participants can then be selective when it comes to choosing which aspects of Enid and Norman they can concentrate on. It may mean considerable divergence from the participant's own personal characteristics.

c) The improvisation above will help to answer this question. Although they have elements of loneliness in common (and lack some of the qualities dealt with in this book?), there is also a contrast: Enid has a more outgoing side to her than Norman, who is preoccupied with his own problems and is a more vulnerable target.

d) During the conversation a picture of Norman's background, etc. will have been building up in Enid's mind. The person playing her has to work out at what point she decides on his age. And how old is Enid herself? It will be interesting to see if the girls' views on this differ from the boys'. She could be older than she appears.

e) In the play Norman and Enid do not have a future. If, however, the participants feel that their relationship can take this, then they will be right.

Questions/suggestions

a) Most of Enid's remarks are questions. What thoughts lie behind each one? And what does she discover?

b) Enact a scene where you deliberately give a false impression:
- to impress someone
- to gain sympathy
- to seem less than you really are

c) What appear to be Norman's and Enid's attitude to each other? And what might they have in common?

d) Enid seems to have worked out Norman's age. Can you? How old do you think Enid is?

e) Do you think that this relationship has a future?

Acknowledgements

The author and publishers would like to thank the following for permission to use copyright material:

Curtis Brown on behalf of the author for 'The Lawn Mower' by June Thomson, copyright © June Thomson, 1970.

Ian Hamilton Finlay for an extract from *Walking Through Seaweed* (Penguin New England Dramatists, 1970).

Lemon Una & Durbridge Ltd. on behalf of the author for an extract from *The Long and the Short and the Tall* by Willis Hall (Penguin, 1961). All rights in this play are strictly reserved and all enquiries for performance, etc. should be made in advance to Lemon Una & Durbridge Ltd., 24 Pottery Lane, Holland Park, London W11 4LZ (tel: 071 727 1346).

Penguin Books Ltd., for extracts from 'Roots' in *The Wesker Trilogy* by Arnold Wesker (Penguin Books, 1959), copyright © Arnold Wesker, 1959, 1960.

The Society of Authors on behalf of the Literary Trustees of Walter de la Mare for 'Old Ben' by Walter de la Mare; and on behalf of the Bernard Shaw Estate for an extract from *Saint Joan* by Bernard Shaw.

Clare Summerfield for 'Windy Boy in a Windswept Tree' by Geoffrey Summerfield, BBC School Broadcast pamphlet, 'Living Language, Spring 1970.

Every effort has been made to trace all the copyright holders, but if any have been inadvertently overlooked the publishers will be pleased to make the necessary arrangements at the first opportunity.